PROCEEDINGS

AT THE

Laying of the Corner Stone

OF THE

SAGE COLLEGE

OF THE

CORNELL UNIVERSITY,

May 15, 1873.

TO WHICH IS ADDED A REPORT TO THE TRUSTEES OF THE CORNELL UNIVERSITY ON THE ESTABLISHMENT OF SAID COLLEGE.

ITHACA:
AT THE UNIVERSITY PRESS.
1873.

PROCEEDINGS

AT THE

Laying of the Corner Stone

OF THE

SAGE COLLEGE

OF THE

CORNELL UNIVERSITY,

May 15, 1873.

TO WHICH IS ADDED A REPORT TO THE TRUSTEES OF THE CORNELL UNIVERSITY ON THE ESTABLISHMENT OF SAID COLLEGE.

ITHACA:
AT THE UNIVERSITY PRESS.
1873.

PROCEEDINGS.

PRAYER BY REVEREND M. C. TYLER.

Most High and Holy God, before whom all darkness is as the light, and all wisdom of man is but darkness, we humbly and joyfully acknowledge thee to be our Creator and Redeemer.

Beneath this open vault, in the broad temple of the world Thou hast made, rejoicing in this genial air and this goodly assemblage of scholars of truth, we bow our hearts and implore thy blessing upon this act of consecration.

We place this stone with reverent hands. From the stately house of learning, which already rises before our vision, from these cloisters, let streams of light and truth and goodness flow for the healing of the world.

Consecrate, we beseech Thee, all those who shall soon throng these halls to the new era of generous and impartial culture. May the generosities of the founders of these halls, be rewarded by the fair and holy characters which shall here be formed; by the modesty and grace which shall adorn true Christian culture; by the endless unfolding of science, philanthropy and piety, in all coming generations.

O God, Fountain of all Love and Wisdom, to whom all human science is but a faint shadow of truth, more and more inspire us with humility, because of our ignorance; and with hope, because of the disclosures still to be made to us.

Praised be thy name for the legacies of past wisdom, for the victories of patient intellect sometimes crowned with martyrdom, and for the Christlike humility and love that have been joined with profoundest learning in the centuries past.

More and more prosper, we beseech thee, all researches of reverent science.

May a holy awe inspire the philosopher, the statesman, the scholar, as Thou art seen to be the inspiration and source of all the laws which thou hast made.

Remove all veils of falsehood, imposture and superstition, from our hearts and minds. Heal all the diseases of human society. Give patience to all who endure unutterable wrongs and oppressions, which come from the ignorance and helplessness of mankind.

Inspire with generous and holy purpose all magistrates and rulers. Purify all senates of legislation, and preserve from corruption and anarchy the cities of the republic. Let the Kingdom of Jesus Christ our Lord be established in all our hearts, and fill the whole earth. Accept us, we beseech Thee; and praise shall be to Father, Son and Spirit evermore! *Amen.*

INTRODUCTORY REMARKS OF PRESIDENT WHITE.

It is now a little more than four years since we met in yonder pleasant village to begin, formally, our work of instruction.

At that time ground was taken, both by our honored Founder in his introductory speech, and by the President of the institution in his inaugural address, in favor of the education of young men and young women together in colleges and universities.

In Mr. Cornell this idea seemed an instinct. He had enjoyed none of the advantages given in seminaries of advanced instruction; he had been too much immersed in business, to have heard much argument for or against perpetuating in the nineteenth century semi-monastic arrangements which suited the thirteenth; there was in him, I think, an instinctive love of fair play, an instinctive distrust of new theories to bolster up outworn practices; and these instincts he expressed in that first official utterance, when he declared his hope that women should be educated here as well as young men.

On the other hand, the ideas expressed that day by the President of the University were founded upon experience and observation within our higher institutions of learning. He had noted the fact that for very many years, in academies, high schools and normal schools, young men and young women of marriageable age, and from distant homes, had been educated together; that while receiving such instruction they had generally been left without surveillance and to their own sense of propriety; that all this had gone on without scandal, without suspicion of danger or wrong, and with such happy results in acquiring knowledge and in the building of character, that of all the men and matrons of this and neighboring States, none are more valued than those educated on this system.

There happened to be in the audience on that day a man who had thought upon this matter more deeply than had either of the speakers. With them it was a goodly theory; with him it was more. He had arrived not only at belief in the justice of admitting young women to our college and universities, but he had come to believe this the natural method—the healthful method—the way out of the disorder, the grossness, the boorishness, which have so long afflicted institutions for the advanced instruction of young men.

Doubtless, too, with this belief was mingled a kindly personal feeling. For, in his boyhood, he had roamed over these hills and along the shores of yonder lake, and among these gorges and forests about us; all this landscape, which has to you merely a wonderful physical beauty, has to him a consecration.

Upon the evening then of that day when we began our work here, this man came to me and said, "when you are ready to carry out the idea of educating young women as thoroughly as young men, I will provide the endowment to enable you to do so." That man was Henry W. Sage.

Time passed on. There was a world of hard work

to do in that first period of organization; there were heavy loads to carry, struggles to go through, plans to work out with infinite painstaking; and our friend's offer waited. But it was never forgotten, and at last the time arrived, and he came forward to redeem his promise. Time had not weakened his determination; it had but served to ripen it. His gift was larger than any of us had dreamed of for such a purpose; and to-day, for this College and yonder Chapel, it stands at three hundred thousand dollars.

The matter was brought before the Trustees of the University, and a committee was appointed to examine and report upon it. I had the honor to be associated with Mr. Sage on that committee, and together we visited various institutions where the experiment had been tried. In due time our report was made. The Trustees accepted the gift and decided to go on with the work.

Among the universities which we visited was one which had been working out this problem of coëducation during about two years—the noblest by far of the universities of the west—one to which this institution of ours looks with respect as an elder sister; nay, as in some sense, a mother. I allude to the University of Michigan. Brief as has been this experiment in her halls, she has reached results of very great importance; and most heartily do I rejoice that her President is with us here to-day, and by his side three others, formerly professors of that institution and now called to responsible positions elsewhere, but all ready to testify as to their experience in this matter.

Since the acceptance of the gift, the work has gone steadily on ; and these massive foundations show that this College building has been well begun. It is the wish of its founder that it be a good building, and I hazard nothing in saying that, with possibly two exceptions, it is the finest among the college buildings of our country. I know of some few more costly ; I know of none more beautiful. I trust that the modesty of our architect, Professor Babcock, will not be offended when I say that he has planned for us a building admirably suited to the founder's noble purpose. Its arrangement of study and sleeping-rooms ; its spacious parlors ; its gymnasium, bath-rooms and infirmary ; its corridor, open to the southern sun and protected from the winds of winter ; its conservatory, its lecture-rooms, laboratory, museum, green-house and botanic garden, for the department of botany and horticulture, and other attractions, all combine to make it a healthful and cheerful students' home.

But comfort and bare utility have not been the only things thought of. As a believer in the possibility of "sermons in stones," I rejoice to see that in and about this building there is to be a great deal of crystallized eloquence, very forcible though very quiet, and moreover, perpetual. These two examples of the work which has come from the hands and brains and hearts of our stone-carvers—these two sculptured capitals—with all their crisp leaves and rich fruits and flowers, are to stand among a multitude of others no less exquisite in workmanship, and they testify to you that while utility and comfort are provided for, there is to be a ministering unto the sense of beauty.

And here I cannot forbear a word of acknowledgment. Among the many services, so good, so kind, so quiet, which have endeared to us Professor Goldwin Smith, not the least is his thoughtfulness in bringing over here a body of workmen, skilled in the best practice, and to some extent trained in the best art-schools, of the mother-country. These beautiful sculptures are their work. They have been done with love, and years after we have passed away they will be looked upon with gratitude.

And now I present to you one whom you will certainly be glad to hear—the man who can most fitly speak here to-day; to you, citizens of Ithaca, I present an old friend; to you, Trustees, Faculty, and students of the University, a benefactor—the Honorable Henry W. Sage.

ADDRESS OF HENRY W. SAGE.

We meet to-day upon this beautiful hillside, to inaugurate an enterprise which I think cannot but have an important influence upon the future of this Commonwealth and of our race.

It has been wisely said that "who educates a woman educates a generation;" and the structure which is to be erected over this corner-stone will be especially devoted to the education of women, and will carry with it a pledge of all the power and resources of Cornell University to "provide and *forever maintain* facilities for the education of women as broadly as for men." This may truly be said to mark a new era in the history of education; for, although the education of women with men has been heretofore practically conducted, notably at Oberlin, Ohio, for many years, and at Ann Arbor, Michigan, for three years past, this is the first University in this country, if not in the world, which has at the same time boldly recognized the rights of woman as well as man to all the education she will ask, and pledged itself to the policy and duty of maintaining equal facilities for both. It is, then, no small matter of congratulation that this University, a State institution, endowed by our general government with a princely gift of lands, and by Ezra Cornell, its founder, with his own fortune, and, more than that, with his own great, earnest heart and zealous love for man, is fairly committed to the education and elevation of woman, and that henceforth the structures now standing here, and those which shall hereafter be added to them, are to be used forever for the education of woman with man, to whom God gave her as an help-meet, and as the mother and chief educator of his race!

I am not one of those who believe that the nature and functions of woman, or her most important sphere of duties in this life, are to be essentially changed by education. God established these from the beginning, and his purposes do not change. But I do most earnestly believe that every power he has given her, that every grace and virtue which adorn her nature, that every element of usefulness and helpfulness to herself and others, may be increased without limit by education and culture, and that, in proportion as these are added to her, will our race be elevated and improved.

But the world has been slow in coming to this conclusion; and during the long centuries since our first parents left Eden, woman, subject to man, has developed less of her natural powers than he. In her moral and affectional nature she has grown, in quality at least, with man. But in the higher ranges of intellectual force and culture, in those creative qualities which have marked the progress of ages in art, in science, in philosophy and in legislation, man has, with rare exceptions, walked alone—woman has *not* been his companion and help-meet. And why? The answer to this question is written upon the statute-books of every civilized nation on earth. Man has used his power over her, to say the least, unwisely and ungenerously. She has been restricted by legislation in her rights of property, in her freedom of action, in her power to elevate herself. Less than thirty years since, in this State, a married woman could not control her own property—not even the wages earned by her own hands. They were her husband's. In many things most essential to her interests and well-being man's legislation made her a nullity.

I charge that this was ungenerous, because it injured

woman without benefiting man; that it was unwise, because any limitations upon the development of woman react, and retard the development of our whole race. But we begin to see light, and to-day I am glad to know that there come up, as from the depths of a great want, voices from the best men and women of all lands, which demand that these old heresies be done away with; that woman shall have all rights which justly belong to her as a human being, and that she shall be improved by education and culture for her duties in life as man is for his. Let us consider for a moment this great want. Among the largest portion of the population of this globe to-day, woman is but the slave and servant of man—doing his drudgery, subject to his will. During her period of youth and beauty, the prey and willing victim of the strongest; ignorant, degraded and brutal as the man who is her master. Yet she is there the mother—the teacher, from her own low level, of the growing race. Looking to the most civilized lands we meet problems, which may well challenge the attention of the philanthropist and the Christian statesman. In Great Britain, the female population exceeds the male by nearly a million and a half! In three of our New England States, the excess is nearly sixty thousand. These results have been produced by emigration, by war, shipwrecks, and the risks and calamities which pertain to the employments of men more than women—causes which will not cease, but continue. Now, looking along the line of these facts to logical results, what do we see? Not long hence, millions of women—enough, were they congregated together, to form respectable States—in excess of men! Human souls organized and equipped with faculties for every function of life, endowed by our Creator with all the feelings, impulses, and passions of humanity, instinct with vital force, and reaching out for legitimate spheres of action, which, for very important elements of their nature, can never be attained! In such conditions of this vast mass of humanity, what necessity for restraints and limitations; for elevation and purity; for the positive control of moral and intellectual forces over those of the gross animal nature! And how can this result be attained? There is but one answer to the question: By that elevation of character, by that broadening and deepening of the whole nature, which comes from Christian culture and education. It will inevitably happen that women in large masses must be dependent upon their own efforts for daily bread, and often, for the support of helpless families. To fit them for these trials and duties, the doors of opportunity must be opened wide. All women should have the liberty to learn what they can, and to do what they have the power to do. There should be no restriction in legislation, none in public opinion, upon a woman's right to sustain herself in any honest calling; and she should, as much as man, be fitted by education to use the faculties God has given her where they will avail her the most.

Heretofore, the employments of self-supporting women have been confined to narrow spheres. The needle, the factory, and domestic service have to a large extent bounded them. But with the advancing strides of civilization, new avenues open, and there is no limit to the field which intelligent, earnest women have before them. In the arts and professions, as teachers, editors and authors, as clerks and saleswomen, accountants and telegraphers, in all the higher mechanical employments, in architectural drawing, and in thousands of the less masculine pursuits which men now monopolize, women, educated for the work, can succeed as well. And there is manly work in this world for every man in it besides! In short, the efficient force of the human race will be multiplied in proportion as woman, by culture and education, is fitted for new and broader spheres of action. And will she be less woman with riper development of all her faculties? As wife and mother, as sister, companion and friend, will she be less true to faith and duty? Is man made dwarf, or giant, by increase of moral and intellectual power? We all know what culture in these directions does for him. It will do no less for woman; and when she is completely emancipated from unjust legal shackles, when she is free as man is to seek her own path in life, wherever led by necessity or duty, hope or ambition, when opportunity and aid for culture in any direction are hers, then may we expect to see woman enlarged, ennobled in every attribute, and our whole race, through her, receive impulsion to a higher level in all things great and good! But this is not the time or place to discuss these questions at length. Brief reference to some of the ideas and motives which underlie this offering of a university education to the women of America is enough for the hour. When this structure shall be completed and ready for its uses, let us look upward and forward for results. And if woman be true to herself, if man be true to woman, and both be true to God, there ought to be from the work inaugurated here this day an outflow which shall bless and elevate all mankind!

The corner stone was then laid by Mrs. Sage with the following words:

"I lay this corner stone, in faith
That structure fair and good
Shall from it rise, and thenceforth come
True christian womanhood."

Professor Babcock, the architect, being called upon, said:—

The contents of the box deposited in the corner stone are as follows:—

1. Parchments bearing the date of the laying of the stone, and the names of the architect and builder.
2. Copies of the *Register*.
3. Laws and documents relating to the University.
4. The *Albany Evening Journal Almanac* of 1873.
5. The *New York Daily Times*.
6. The Ithaca daily papers.
7. *The Era*.
8. A letter addressed by Mr. Cornell "To the Coming Man and Woman."

President White:—The corner stone of the Sage

College is now duly laid; may God's blessing rest upon the college, upon its benefactors, upon all who throng its walls, upon all who go forth from it! I have now the pleasure of introducing the gentleman who has written the letter, which has been deposited in the stone, to the coming man and the coming woman. I trust it may be a very long time before that letter comes to its address. I have the very great honor and pleasure of introducing the Honorable Ezra Cornell, who will now address you.

REMARKS OF MR. CORNELL.

Mr. President, Ladies and Gentlemen:—

You will not expect me to undertake to do what I am so little qualified to do—to make a speech; but I rise with pleasure to thank God and our friends, in the name of the Trustees of Cornell University, that this great work goes steadily forward.

Four years ago we met and incorporated the Cornell University. There was a doubt, at least, whether there was not a majority of our Trustees, and a majority of the Faculty that had then been selected for the University, opposed to this work. I cannot say that this was the fact, but it is difficult also for me to say that it was not the fact.

The work is moving forward; and I am now able to assure you that at least a majority, and a very decided majority, of both the Trustees and the Faculty, are in favor of this great experiment; and as for myself, I have the utmost confidence in its success. I regard it as the most important experiment that could be made, not only for the institution, but for our surrounding country. It is important to the citizens of Ithaca, that this experiment should be a successful one; and those of my fellow citizens who are within the hearing of my voice, I trust will bear in mind that much depends upon them for securing the success of this undertaking, and I hope and trust that whatever they may do, they will do most heartily and cheerfully to secure that success.

Again thanking our friends for the means that have enabled us to make this rapid progress in this matter of coëducation, and of placing the women of America upon the same footing with the men of America in regard to education, I will close, with the remark that the letter deposited in the corner stone addressed to the future man and woman, of which I have kept no copy, will relate to future generations the cause of the failure of this experiment, if it ever does fail, as I trust in God it never will.

SPEECH OF ALEXANDER WINCHELL, L.L. D., CHANCELLOR OF THE SYRACUSE UNIVERSITY.

Mr. President:—I felicitate myself heartily in being called upon to participate in the ceremonies of this occasion, the first instance in which a great and prosperous University has so far recognized the imperious demands of the age for equal rights to women, as to lay the corner stone of an edifice to be consecrated especially to their collegiate education. I do this with especial satisfaction, recalling the period spent in professional companionship with him under whose administration this auspicious event takes place, in an institution where for some years he was one of my colleagues, a great and leading university of the west, and one of the greatest and most respectable in the country.

I have long desired to visit this spot, and to tread the soil that has been consecrated to the necessities and uses of Cornell University, a very Minerva among the colleges of the land; but I never anticipated the opportunity to do so would bring with it the opportunity to testify before an audience like this, to my deep interest in the Cornell University, and my hearty good wishes for its welfare, its usefulness, its perpetuity and its greatness.

You remember, Mr. President, when we were associated together as fellow professors, each in his way trying to interpret the records of the past, the question of higher coëducation of men and women used sometimes to be canvassed. At an earlier period, if my recollection serves me rightly, than that which witnessed our association together as fellow professors, the question had been canvassed by the board of regents and professors in the university, and a judgment arrived at, for the time being, adverse to the admission of women into the university. I cannot refrain however, from doing myself the justice to say, that at a period still antecedent to the epoch of that memorable discussion I had myself taken sides with the party, which then constituted the minority in the institution, that was destined so soon to present a strong and respectable majority that should act, and consummate in that action a deed of justice to the other sex. Even at that early period, in surveying the intimations of the time—and I am carried back over an interval of twelve or fifteen years in referring to these events —I had detected as I thought, this great question looming up in the educational horizon, a question which was destined to demand a solution ; but I did not surmise that it would so soon attain to the actual zenith, and overshadow all of us to such an extent that no man can possibly ignore its presence. More than one, I am happy to say, has entertained a conviction upon this subject, which has not been produced by the successes that have been attained in the modern experiments at coëducation, and not produced by events of the magnitude, and importance, and meaning of those which are transpiring to day. Although my own mind has been long settled, and though many minds have been satisfied in regard to the merits of this question, it may be worth the while to suggest to those who are disposed thus to consider the *pros* and *cons* of the argument, that there are certain negative propositions, in the first place, well calculated to dispel all the difficulties that have beset the pathway of those who have been slow to arrive at the conclusion which I have embraced, and have insisted upon on more than one occasion.

Among these negative propositions let it be remembered, in the first place, that this question of the higher coëducation of man and woman is not one which is to be settled as a question of masculine taste. Whether a certain class of men approve or disapprove of the attempt of women to the realities of a university education, has no pertinence to the question. Whether woman possesses the actual right to avail herself of all the advantages that are provided in human society to attain to the highest possible education and culture, is something which has no connection whatever with the prejudices, or opinions, or judgment, of any fragment or portion of masculine humanity. We may like or dislike to see a woman pursuing differential calculus, or translating Homer. We may think it unfeminine, but we have no more right to deny her the privilege, than we have to curtail the right of any man to pursue a vocation which we regard as a violation of good taste or propriety, or as totally at variance with the cast of his mind.

And then, in the next place, the settling of this question in the affirmative does not imply that all women must attain to, or seek after, a collegiate education. No; make what provision we will, there will yet be left an abundance of women to preserve in themselves all that charming mood of nature which we witness in those unsophisticated by Greek and conic sections; a sufficient number to perpetuate all the pretty affectations and unnaturalnesses of the boarding-school miss; and a sufficient number to save us from the awful darkness of ignorance of the New York and Parisian fashions; and a plenty of women to pay homage at the shrine of Madam Demorest.

Neither, in the third place, does it follow, or settle this question in the affirmative, that women, because educated and cultured, are therefore to aspire to political and public stations, and to participate in public life. We may entertain what opinion we will respecting the fitness of women for such positions, respecting those women who aspire to such positions, and respecting the competency of women to discharge high public duties, but all this is foreign to the question, and does not affect her natural dowry in the right to education.

And neither, in the next place, is it pertinent to the question to inquire whether the pursuit of the higher studies be compatible with the health of woman. She is to be her own judge in that respect. We allow her to judge in regard to the healthfulness of all other pursuits. The pursuit of fashion, in some instances, is reported to have been damaging if not ruinous to health; yet in our legislative halls, and in the formation of public opinion, we enact no laws which interfere with the right she exercises to pursue her business of fashion, and to lead a life which may be, and is, prejudicial to her physical health.

Finally, neither are we to enquire whether woman

is capable of competing with her fellow man in the pursuit of higher education. It may be that she will prove an unequal competitor. It may be that she will fall behind, but the only question which concerns us is, does she aspire to this education? Does she desire to associate herself with her brother, her fellow student, in the advanced walks of linguistic and scientific attainments? She has asserted in our ears that such is her aspiration, and we have only to inquire what is the fact in this respect. All these collateral inquiries are entirely foreign to the question of culture of the mind, and we must in justice, concede to woman seeking this privilege—aspiring to enrich her mind with a knowledge of literature and science—the same privileges, the same opportunities, that have been provided so wisely and so generously for our sons and brothers. And there are certain affirmative propositions well calculated to strengthen the convictions of those who have taken sides in the behalf of women on this great question of higher coëducation, to which let me direct your thoughts.

In the first place, the pursuit of the higher literature and science has a tendency to conserve all that is truly feminine in women. We have always maintained that it is the especial office and function of learning and culture to refine. We have always maintained that there is nothing unrefining in the most difficult scientific and literary attainments. The influence of that culture must be the same upon woman as upon man. It must tend to add refinement to the feminine graces and accomplishments which nature has given to women.

That we have seen masculine educated women we must confess, and masculine educated women who in some of their qualities were not especially inviting; but let it be remembered that their masculine cast of character was given to them by nature, and not by the culture which they get in the college or university. Nature is to be charged with that coarseness and roughness, which exist in spite of culture. There are educated men and women who still remain rough and unpolished, but less rough and less unpolished than if they had not received a higher education.

In the next place, I would remind you that the pursuit of science is eminently healthful; and if a woman has, by the laws of nature, a predisposition to debility or invalidism, I am sure that the degree of activity, the bodily and mental action, which we find to be necessary in the pursuit of natural science especially, is a remedy for that tendency. These health-giving influences, which are derived from the pursuit of science, woman has a right to demand for herself. Mr. President, I have not turned back to a time in our experience and in the history of the University of Michigan, when we were enabled to contrast the excuses for absence which were rendered by male and female students on account of sickness, but I might have done so. Before I leave that point, however, I will not refrain from making allusion to the fact that it is well understood by professors and teachers that while many excuses are rendered by young men, who on account of sickness are unable to attend the exercises, and when those excuses come to us, we are in the habit of accepting them, believing those students to be honorable young men, and not entertaining for a moment a doubt as to the truth of their statements or the validity of their excuses; there is something entirely remarkable in the fact that excuses of this kind, in our experience in the University of Michigan, came less frequent from the female side of the University than from the other. Does not that argue that a healthy influence is exerted by the pursuit of higher studies? We have found hard study and severe study to be entirely compatible with female physical vigor. The college, I believe, may be put in favorable contrast with the boarding-school in this respect.

In the next place, I would remind you as one of my affirmative propositions, that woman is a success in the pursuit of science. My thoughts turn back to my experience as a student in schools and academies preparatory to college. Perhaps I was in a mood to be unduly impressed as to the excellencies of the other sex, but there is certainly one thing I have a faint recollection of, and that is, that the most penetrating and successful student, with the most comprehensive grasp of the subject which I ever saw, in that dread and horror of college students, the differential calculus, was a lady. She was a little my senior, and it is in this way that I account for her superiority over myself.

And I remember, too, of being in a class where there were young ladies who were pursuing the study of geometry; and the neatest, and readiest, and most convincing demonstrations of propositions in geometry came from those fair and charming lips.

And then you remember, Mr. President and friends, that the history of the world has given us many names of women prominent in science and literature. History gives us the name of Hypatia, a teacher of philosophy in the Platonic school of Alexandria; and you will remember also, how in later times, in the middle ages, the University of Bologna served itself with female professors, and furnished the world such an array of names of illustrious ladies, as to give to that renowned university a lustre which is destined to be perpetuated through all time. Laura Bassi was a professor of mathematics and natural philosophy in that university, and gave learned lectures attended by crowds of learned women as well as men, in the pursuit of the higher sciences, from the surrounding countries, from France and Germany; and you well remember how this lady attained to such distinction in the world of letters and science, as to be honored with the degree of Doctor of Laws. There is also the name of Novella d'Andrea, professor of astronomy, who, by skill in mathematics, and by the the delivery of learned lectures, attained to a position of celebrity that has never been surpassed; and the name of Maria Agnesi, professor of mathematics, who occupied the chair that had previously been occupied by her father. In linguistic science and literature, Clotilde Tambroni, a professor of Greek, and other eminent women, reflect equal lustre upon the history of the University of Bologna, while in France, Madam Dacier was the distinguished editress of some of the Greek classics of the celebrated Delphin edition. And among the literary and learned ladies to whom we might refer, we recall such names as that of Mrs. Mary Somerville, who was latterly almost the peer and compeer of the celebrated mathematician and astronomer Laplace; of Caroline Herschel, the distinguished assistant and colaborer of her more distinguished brother Sir William Herschel, who has testified that but for her coöperation, and the services she rendered him in the pursuit of astronomical science, he could not have attained the results which crowned his life.

In our own country, as some of the more advanced students in botany will remember, there is the name of Mrs. Almira Lincoln Phelps, the author of a text book on botany, which has continued in use in our schools for a longer period than any text book ever introduced to the American public; and Miss Youmans, another ornament to botanical science; and Miss Redfield who was an expert in zoölogical science, and also an author; and Mrs. Agassiz, the wife of the non-resident professor of zoölogy in this institution. I need but mention the name of this thorough scholar and charming writer, to convince you that women are capable of attaining to as consummate a degree of knowledge and culture in zoölogical science as any man in the country. Lastly, Miss Mitchell, professor in the department of astronomy, is worthy to be named in connection with the female professors of astronomy in other and foreign institutions.

In my own experience, Mr. President, to which you did me the honor to allude, I have had an opportunity to make observations which are similarly convincing. A few years ago, as has been remarked, ladies were for the first time admitted to Michigan University; and I am able to testify that they have acquitted themselves with just as much credit to themselves, as have the men who studied with them. A few years ago, the first year I think when women entered in any numbers, I had the pleasure of instructing a class of one hundred and two in botany, and at the close of the period of instruction, a written examination was had, and in looking over the examination papers I paid particular attention to the characteristics of these papers in reference to the subject matter which had been treated of, and in reference to the correctness of the spelling of technical terms, and I am very happy to announce the fact, that in both of these respects the lady members of the class stood number one. I would say, however, in order to make this statement clearer and more forcible, that I entered into an analysis of the different groups of persons constituting the class. There were first I may say the ladies, then the gentlemen constituting the class. It was made up also of regular freshmen. (Laughter). Yes, regular freshmen and irregular freshmen, and among the freshmen were the classical students and scientific students, and in addition to the freshmen there were also select students, and pharmacy students, and irregular students —I mean irregular in their studies. The class was classified with reference to residence, whether as residents of Michigan or non-residents; they were also divided according to course, into classical, latin-scientific, and scientific, or classical and non-classical; and so I made out of this list of one hundred and two persons seventeen groups, and however I could group them the ladies always stood first. Now it may be pertinent for me to make a few other statements in this connection, and as they are of interest, and as they may be made the text for some very interesting discussion if any one shall ever take them up, I will read an abstract of the other results.

Taking the several groups in the order of proficiency, and giving only the percentage of perfection in the character of their examination papers, we obtain the following exhibits:—Female freshmen 93; latin-scientific freshmen, including some females 97; all classical students 75; all Michigan freshmen 74; all Michigan students 73; foreign freshmen 72; classical freshmen 72; the whole body of freshmen 71; all students examined 71; select students 70; foreign students 70; male freshmen 70; all non-classical students 69; scientific freshmen 68; pharmacy students 66; foreign non-freshmen 65; Michigan non-freshmen, last of all, 60.

Now I do not mean to imply, friends, that the attainments of the gentlemen in this class were low, absolutely, but rather that the proficiency of the ladies was high absolutely. Neither do I imply that this disparity in the relative proficiency existing between the two sexes is something destined to be maintained in the whole history of the university. I admit that these ladies who stood this test were a select class of lady students; only that class of ladies had then ventured to make application for admission to the university. Hereafter, when the average lady student shall be emboldened by the success of these to knock at the door of the University and find admittance, I expect we shall find an equality in the scholastic merits of the two sexes. Be that as it may, my observations upon this class, and similar observations upon a larger class, which I taught about a year ago, of two hundred students, convinced me, and, as I believe demonstrated, that women are capable of pursuing the study of science successfully and creditably. But whether they can or cannot succeed, as I before asserted, it is their right to be there, and to do the best they can.

Now in concluding these remarks, allow me to echo some sound advice which fell upon my ears recently from the lips of a most distinguished American educator: "*Follow after truth—follow after the whole truth.*" In laying the foundation and rearing the superstructure of this edifice, and of this institution whose corner stone we put in place to-day, let no department of the domain of truth be neglected. Let the minds of those who shall be trained here be enriched with the knowledge of truth in all its integrity; let it be remembered that the field of moral and religious truth, and the moral and religious history of our race at large, supply us with the data and basis of a philosophy as positive as any drawn from the facts of physics, or of civil history; that these women who shall flock to this building have the right to have their education directed to the entire field of truth, and to be reminded that it is the will of the Author of truth, that the entire field shall be faithfully and candidly explored.

As truth is an expression of the mind and will and thought of God, so are mere unreasoning human dogmas, and narrow prejudices, both irreverent towards God and unworthy of one who takes upon himself the sacred office of giving instruction to man or woman in the truth which God has ordained to be.

The next speaker was Moses Coit Tyler, editor of the Christian Union, and formerly Professor of the University of Michigan.

SPEECH OF MOSES COIT TYLER.

Mr. President, Ladies and Gentlemen:—It is the remark of one of the true thinkers of our time, Frederick Robertson, that the first maxim in conduct and in culture is this; "Save yourself from all sectarianism." And what is sectarianism, in any direction, but the imperfectness of doing things by sections rather than by spheres, partially rather than integrally?

In this vast and fatal business of education, particularly the higher education, has not the world all the while been held back, and human growth cramped and stifled, by the pettiness of educational sectarianism; that is, by the adoption in education of principles viewed only on one side, and of methods fragmentary in execution?

There, to begin with, is the educational sectarianism which takes limited and prejudiced conceptions of the topics upon which education should be employed. It fences off a certain small section of knowledge, and sprinkles upon it the drops of its consecration, and then says to the young student: "There is your true field of work. There only should you delve and plough and gather your harvest." The first sectary who meets us in this spirit, perhaps, is the classical sectary, and he says: "Only the dead words that were once alive and musical in the streets of Athens and of Rome are worthy of the scholar's devotion." But just behind him, and with equal intensity, cries out another: "Only the literatures of living speech, and not the dead ones at all, are worthy of living men." But these voices are soon drowned in the vehement exclamations of a third sectary, not at all less confident than the others: "Why fritter life away," he says, "over mere words—mouthfuls of spoken wind? Give us something tangible and practical in education. What you call literary studies are but a waste of time and force upon vapid and fruitless tasks. Of course, in this practical age, science furnishes the only education which is of any real utility."

So, everywhere, the sectaries in education grapple together, and rend each other with mutual reproaches, —each one making his own private partiality in knowledge the test and the measure of all desirable knowledge. Accordingly, since institutions of learning have commonly been founded under the guidance of such men, we find here one school dedicated to one bit of knowledge, and there another school reared to the service of another bit of knowledge; but, at last, the truth has begun to dawn upon us, that schools which teach only bits of knowledge, at least do not deserve to be called universities. That school, only, is the university, where the universe of knowledge is cherished and pursued.

But educational sectarianism shows itself in another form, not less disagreeable than the other, and of more particular interest for us here to-day. This is the form of sectarianism which applies itself, not to the studies to be pursued, but to the students who are to pursue them; which throws its limitations about persons and not about topics; which belittles not the area of knowledge, but the number of those who may have access to knowledge; and which does this on principles that are unreasonable and unjust. For, in all this world, what is there that ought to be freer to all who hunger for it than knowledge, which, as a great lover of it said three hundred years ago, "bringeth to every kinde of man the truest pleasur, the surest profet, the greatest praise that can be either gotten in earth or given from heaven (heaven only excepted)"? What cruelty, therefore, is more cruel, what exclusiveness is more unnatural, than that which would bar out from this exquisite and supreme boon, any human being who is qualified to partake of it? Yet we know that in times past just this has been done; we know that in times present just this is still done.

To say nothing of those cases of exclusion from the university, which have rested on matters of creed or race, this must be mentioned, that nearly all the greatest, most respectable, and most advantageous universities in the world to-day make the fact that a student—however gifted with abilities, however accomplished in studies, however fine and noble in character—is a woman, the ground for her being denied all the incomparable intellectual benefits of which they have accumulated the trust in the course of ages, and of which they hold a sort of monopoly; thus virtually repelling from the higher pursuits of knowledge those who would be among the most loyal and most successful seekers of it, and thus adding to this original cruelty the secondary one of giving encouragement to the insolent taunt, which says either that high learning is impossible to a woman, or else that it is unbecoming in her.

For my part, I think that the deepest significance of this rare festival which is enacted here to-day is, that it is a protest—a benign, let us hope an efficacious protest—against this most arbitrary species of educational sectarianism. It is a proclamation that at last, here, on these beautiful and bountiful heights, the entire circle of catholicity in education is to be rounded out to its fullness. This festival signifies that, in the invitation which the University sends abroad into the world, there shall no longer remain any discord of inconsistency to jar the magnanimous words of its Founder, who would have this a place "where any person can get instruction in any study." This, indeed, seems to be the true idea of a university—a school, in its instruction as universal as knowledge, and in its invitation as universal as the lovers and seekers of knowledge. To throw open all studies to the free choice of all human beings,—that is the only scheme for a University worthy of this ground we stand on, and of the period of time which the world has grown to.

I am sure, therefore, that we are all glad and proud to be here to participate in the inspiration of this most memorable scene. We are all glad to have the privilege, on this very spot, of joining in this living testimony of thanks to Mr. Sage, the wise and large-hearted benefactor who rears here this temple, not of education only, but of educational justice likewise; and whose name, from the rocky seed which he now plants in this soil, will reap harvests of benediction through all times to come.

It would be hard to imagine any misfortune in manners or in morals—or in civilization, that larger something which includes both manners and morals—more serious than would follow from a wide and palpable disparity in the culture of the sexes. But who does not see, in the enormous multiplication of colleges and in the great diffusion of the desire and the ability to go to them, that a liberal education is to be the rule and not the exception for the gentleman of the future —that "Coming Man" to whom Mr. Cornell wrote the letter which he has just deposited in yonder corner stone? But unless a liberal education be likewise the rule and not the exception for the lady of the future —the "Coming Woman" who is also addressed by Mr. Cornell's letter—both lady and gentleman will associate, in the future, in a companionship that will have elements of inevitable misunderstanding and embarrassment for both. "Women and men," says John Stuart Mill, "at last are companions; unless she rises, he sinks."

Besides all this, in man's efforts towards any great achievement in this world, he never works so gracefully, never so wisely, never so successfully, as when he has the company and the help of woman. We are all glad, therefore, to be here to exchange congratulations over this act, in which man not only confers blessing upon woman, but confers blessing upon himself also; for he thus secures to the extent here possible, the company and the help of woman in the greatest task he has in this world—the prosecution of knowledge, which Lord Bacon calls that "great Plea or Suit, granted by the Divine favor and providence, whereby the human race seeks to recover its right over nature."

I have just spoken the name of Lord Bacon. It

seems to me that in a university like this, there is no other name more fit to be spoken than the name of that prodigious man whose mind was itself a sort of university—for had he not taken all knowledge for his province?—and whose philosophy has reformed the old universities and established the new ones, and still lives in all our best studies—commanding us with unceasing monition, to keep our faces fronting "the true end of knowledge," which is "the glory of God and the relief of man's estate." So I need make no apology for quoting here, as I conclude these remarks, still another saying of this master of us all, this perpetual chancellor of all the liberal universities. As will be recollected by everyone, it was in Lord Bacon's day that Galileo invented the telescope, and pointed it for the first time, with eager and reverent expectation, toward the infinite mysteries of the sky. You know what a revelation rewarded that first real look into the heavens; and as the message announcing it sped across the bosom of Europe, from land to land, to the few wise men who were anywhere waiting to hear it, it found in England one man, perhaps only one man, already with hand upon ear to catch its import from afar. That man was Lord Bacon. And when he heard what Galileo had done, he pronounced it an achievement *dignum humano genere*. And, sir, while sitting here this afternoon, I have been trying to think what word would be the most fitting by which to describe the act which takes visible form here to-day. I might say that it is worthy of Henry W. Sage to do this thing.

That would be true. I might say that the doing of this thing is worthy of Cornell University, and of its munificent founder. That would be true; for in the very midst of the grave charges against Mr. Cornell which now fill even the air we breathe, I desire to express my individual belief, based on good evidence, that these charges are wantonly and entirely false. And again I might say, that the doing of this thing is worthy of the President of Cornell University—a man who, when the whole world shall come to know him as his own friends already know him, will be as distinguished for self-sacrifice as he even now is distinguished for brilliant ability. Yet it seems to me that the best language by which to characterize the foundation, upon this spot, under all the circumstances of our time, of the Sage College for Women, would be simply to say of it in the comprehensive phrase of Lord Bacon, that it is an achievement worthy of human nature. And if it be so, who can have any doubt of the result?

REMARKS OF PROFESSOR GOLDWIN SMITH.

Mr. President, for the first and probably for the last time in my life, I am rather glad to be called upon, although I never rise among American speakers without the most painful conciousness of my English defects. I have made a point of being here to-day.

With regard to the special object of this meeting, I have three things to say. First, that I heartily pay homage to the munificence and benevolence of the founder of this edifice. I pay a respect in which no flattery or insincerity mingles, an unfeigned respect, to any rich man who can keep his heart above his wealth and remain true to humanity. In the second place, let me say that no man connected with the cause of education, can be more heartily desirous for the improvement and education of women than I am. We have, on my side of the line, set on foot a movement in the form of ladies' classes, in which I have been most happy to take part ever since I have been in Canada. I would only say, that in removing artificial privileges and artificial barriers, let us take care that we do not attempt to remove the great land marks of nature, or encourage in the sexes the belief that they are rival competitors, instead of being helpmates.

In the third place, let me say that upon any doubtful question connected with education, I should pay sincere deference to the opinion of the President and the Faculty of this University. I have passed some years in intercourse with the President and the members of the Faculty, and I have a sincere respect for their opinion, and shall be sincerely inclined to defer to them on any question when my opinion might differ from theirs; and I was glad to gather from Mr. Cornell's remarks that the Faculty, as well as the Trustees, had been consulted upon this important question, and that this measure has their approbation.

My chief reason for wishing to be present here to-day, and for giving up another engagement to be present, was that I might gratify my own personal feelings by appearing among the friends of Cornell University. I understand that it has been said by people who have nothing more important to talk about, that I had lost hope in the University and had deserted it. I am unwilling that, to the misconstruction under which the rules of this Institution labor, there should be added even so trifling a misconstruction as that. I have not lost hope in the Cornell University, nor have I deserted it; my hopes for it and my affections for it are unchanged. My home, which for three very happy years was among the kind hearted citizens of Ithaca, is now in Canada. There are my relatives, probably the nearest relatives I have; and besides, it is natural that an English citizen should be most at home under the English flag.

The President has adverted to the time when I and my friend John Stuart Mill, who has just passed from among us, and Bright and other political friends were struggling in England in favor of the Union of the United States. Throughout that struggle, I had what I thought was the real honor of my own country in view; and I have never ceased to be an Englishman, as probably the readers of the American press have some reason to know. My home is in Canada, but I retain the connection which I have had from the beginning with this University. My affections for it are unchanged, my hopes for it are unabated.

I will not say that it has no difficulties still to contend with. It will still need wise and prudent government, as all are aware, who are aware of the immense difficulty of building up a great institution, and above all a great university. It will need wise government, in order that it may have its resources steadily directed, not towards objects of display, but toward solid and essential objects. It will need to be cautious how it ventures on perilous experiments. It will need to have permanently attached to it, and untired in their devotion, a staff of able and energetic professors. All this it will need, nor can any one yet exactly predict what form the institution will ultimately take; but I believe it will be a great and good institution, and one which any man will feel it an honor to serve. I have believed it an honor to serve it, and I hope that I shall still feel it to be an honor.

I was especially anxious to be present to-day, in order to show that those suspicions which are abroad, and which have taken form in calumnious charges, have no presence in my mind. It is not for me to meet the attacks that have been made upon the founder of this University. No doubt proper investigation will take place, and those attacks be refuted in a most decisive manner. It is not for me, a foreigner and a stranger, to trace such calumnies to local, political, or personal causes. But in this Government of faction, of which we are all enamored and believe to be the only best government for man, among other faults is that of slander; and that is the bane of other countries besides the United States. Morever, let me say this: That though I feel it is an honor to serve this University, and that no doubt, no cloud which might pass over its prosperity, would in the least degree influence my mind, I would not serve it for a moment if I had the slightest suspicion that it was devoted to any other than a public object, or that it was in the slightest degree, or in the most indirect manner, promoting private gain.

I am, of course, not officially cognizant of its affairs; but I have lived in an atmosphere of the warmest friendship with the President, and he has told me plainly and without any reservation, of his difficulties, and of all that was going on. I have met, too, and conversed upon this subject with persons who were opponents to Cornell, and unfavorable to this institution, and they also, I am sure, speak without reserve; and let me assure you that I am perfectly convinced, as convinced as I am of my own existence, that the management of the property of the University has been wholly for the benefit of the University, and strictly in accordance with the rules of honor.

I do not choose to flatter Mr. Cornell. I believe that flattery is the greatest insult you can offer to a man of any sense, or any depth of character; but I am perfectly convinced of his unselfishness, and perfectly convinced that, when an investigation takes place, his name will come out as pure as the driven snow. Errors he may have committed in the execution of so difficult and complicated a task, and one requiring so much experience; but depend upon it that he is innocent of these things which are charged upon him; that his hands are clear, his aims are unselfish, his character is pure; and that no one who serves Cornell University need fear that he is serving anything but the cause of humanity.

Ladies and Gentlemen, I will say no more.

SPEECH OF COLONEL HOMER B. SPRAGUE.

Fifty years ago, Mrs. Emma Willard, whose name is worthy to be enrolled with those of the foremost educators of modern times, established at Waterford, N. Y., a female seminary. At her first public examination, a young lady recited so well in geometry that many of the listeners were incredulous, and some declared that it was a mere act of memory, for they said that no woman ever did or ever could learn geometry.

At that time, the subject of an advanced and thorough education for females in science and in literature was new, and its advocacy somewhat alarming. Even Mrs. Willard is careful not to shock publie sentiment by any bold innovation. She endeavors to disarm prejudice, by saying that she has no idea of giving to girls a real college education. On her petition to the legislature for aid, she enters her *caveat* in these remarkable words: "The absurdity of sending ladies to college will strike every one, and I hasten to say, that the seminary which I propose will be as different from those appropriated to the other sex, as the female character and duties are from the male." Year after year she pressed her plan upon the attention of the Assembly, and her efforts were heartily seconded by that enlightened statesman, Gov. DeWitt Clinton, who, in one of his messages recommending the scheme, says: "It is the only attempt ever made in the United States to promote the education of females by the patronage of the government." But it failed.

This was the first female academy in the United States. It afterwards grew into that noble institution, *The Troy Female Seminary.* There appears to have been at that time no high school for girls, much less any female college. For twenty years, that is, till 1839, there was no normal school in the country. Indeed, the prevalent ideas on the subject of female education were heathenish.

In Greece it has been confined to the *hetaerae*, a class of whom the least said the better. In Rome, except with some of the patricians and afterwards with a few christians, it was very uncommon. In China, it is still what it was twenty thousand years ago, when roast pig was invented in the days of Ho-ti, as recorded by Charles Lamb; every Chinese boy is taught to read and write; but no girl, except occasionally a daughter of the rich. They belittle her mind, as they do her foot. The Hindoo women are Caspar Hausers, buried body and soul in their zenanas. The Turk gravely denies that woman has a soul. A

Christian writer of the thirteenth century, evidently the parent of a long line, defines appropriate female education in his day, as instructing her "to pray to God, to love man, to knit, and to sew."

What a change! The progress of physical science has hardly been more marvellous within the last generation, than the progress of ideas on the right education of this half of the human race. The census of 1870 and the report of the Commissioner of education show in the United States nearly one hundred thousand high schools, one hundred and forty normal schools, and more than fifteen hundred academies. To a large majority of these institutions young ladies are as freely admitted as young gentlemen, and in about equal numbers. The same public documents show us fifty-four colleges for females, and seventy-seven into which both sexes are admitted. I am well aware that some of these exist on paper only. Indeed, it requires a vivid and creative imagination to take a score of children, call them freshmen, sophomores, juniors, and seniors, dub the school-ma'am "President and Faculty," take away thebirch rod and substitute the power of expulsion, give the urchins diplomas in barbarous Latin instead of yellow rewards-of-merit in good English, and style the whole thing a College instead of Kindergarten, or a University instead of a district school. So intangible and mystical are some of these "colleges," that the Commissioner of education, acute and painstaking as he is, cannot ascertain n eighty-five of them, what is the *sex* of the students.

But making all due abatement for ambitious and poetical exaggeration, it is clear that the experiment of higher education for females has been very extensively tried.

What has been the result? The testimony of these institutions is multitudious and it is uniform, showing that the female intellect is equal to the male. My own experience is a fair illustration. It embraces high-schools, of which I had charge for years, and in which, among many excellent scholars in Greek, Latin, Mathematics, some of whom now occupy distinguished positions, the best scholar was a young lady; a normal school, in which the ladies were fully equal to the gentlemen; and an incorporated academy, of which I have now had charge for nearly three years, containing more than five hundred students, of whom the girls, though largely inferior in number, carry off most of the prizes. So far as the experience of the hundreds of educational institutions of all grades, from the high school to the university, during more than a quarter of a century, could solve what is problematic, or settle what is *a priori* likely, it has established the fact that in the United States young women are at least equally capable with young men.

I hail this result. Admit it, and you must admit the desirableness of such institutions as this whose corner stone we have just laid. Deny it, and you only strengthen the argument by showing the greater need of them

It is objected that there is no demand for advanced

female education. So much the worse for our civilizathon, for there is hardly a surer test. But is it true that there is no demand? Possibly, the call may not be so general or so urgent as we could wish. Froude tells us that a great man must create a taste for himself. Very likely, people must be educated to appreciate education. But surely, the spontaneous upspringings of thousands of schools which profess to give high instruction to ladies demonstrates the existence of a great and growing demand, and, if anything could emphasize the fact and intensify its significance, it would be a scene like this.

I do not deny the wide prevalence of a feeling, a relic of the old barbarism, a vague impression, very general among the unthinking, that woman less needs education than man. One fact, a result and evidence of this, is seen in the revelation of the last census, that of three million adults in our country unable to read and write, there are one hundred and forty-five illiterate women to every hundred illiterate men. On this subject, as on some others, the Sage College will throw light.

It reminds us that learning is good for its own sake. It challenges us to adduce any consideration showing that education is beneficial for one half of the world that will not show it to be equally beneficial for the other half. It reminds us that greater knowledge and higher culture tend ever to nobler character; to give a mastery not only over the outer but over the inner; to subordinate the animal and enthrone the spiritual;

to lift above the brute and brutish appetite, above the savage and savage passion; to enlarge, invigorate, purify, ennoble; to open new fields of useful activity and new sources of refined enjoyment.

Now, why should woman stop just where man begins? Why should the entrance upon a college course for him mark the limit of training for her, and his starting-point be her goal. I know the old, fashionable, mock-chivalric treatment of this subject, the feeble and pretty affectation, which patronizingly regards her as an impossible compound of mental weakness and moral strength, a divine infant, a celestial simpleton, a sick angel. Pope's estimate may be compressed into two words, "Pretty Polly"; Addison's, "Be a good girl; you shall have a new fan." A fashionable poet tells us, "her whole empire is to please." Mrs. Browning happily hits off some of these namby-pambyisms, where, in Aurora Leigh, she makes Romney compliment with polished sarcasm the newly-published book of some fair authoress,

> "Expressing the comparative respect
> Which means the absolute scorn. Oh, excellent!
> What grace! What facile turns! What fluent sweeps!
> What delicate discernment! . . . almost thought!
> The book does honor to the sex, we hold.
> Among our female authors we make room
> For this fair writer, and congratulate
> The country that produces in these times
> Such women—competent to . . . spell!"

If woman's mental constitution be different from man's, surely this University, with its many parallel courses existing and to be established, may happily meet her different needs.

But it will hardly be claimed that her mental constitution is more different than her physical. Why should she have different intellectual, any more than different bodily food? She is an ethereal creature, says the undergraduate poet. Well, must she sip aesthetic tea, just taste the froth and foam, the jellies and cream, the ambrosia and nectar of literature, nibble at homeopathic morsels of science, and, remembering that "every part strengthens a part," feed on the tongues of nightingales and the brains of humming-birds?

I think it is generally admitted that she has a talent for speech. Let her study words, explore, gather, collate, classify the germs, trace their wondrous growths, and see them expand into organic forms and great trees. She has taste and fancy. Let her cull from universal literature the flowers of rhetoric, the aroma of poetry, and create what she does not find. She has memory and insight. Let her summon up the distant past, disentangle historical truth, reproduce and paint the scenes. She has imagination, intuition, and reason. Let her scale the heights of philosophy, gaze into the depths of theology, penetrate the arcana of nature, sift and test the star-dust, track the comet to his fiery lair,

> "And mark faint nebulæ circling into worlds."

The fact is, she needs advanced education as much more than man does as her bodily strength is inferior.

The struggle for existence grows sharper. He can gain a livelihood by animal power. He can dig, lift, drag, carry, fight; wield the oar, the scythe, the flail, the axe, the sword; as your Ithaca poet sings, he

> "Shall swing the hammer in the gleaming mine,
> And plant the ocean with his commerce sails,
> And whirl his engines through the tunneled rock."

But what shall become of his mother, wife, sister, daughter, if driven to toil with her hands? She must rather be able to rely on mind, not muscle; strokes of the pen rather than of the arm; skill, grace, learning, intellect, rather than bone, sinew, brawn, brute force.

More than ever before, she needs this higher training, because new mental activities are opening to her. There is the vast field of authorship. In 1824 Mrs. Child, on the publication of her first book, was warned that thenceforward she could not be considered respectable, because she had written a book! But who sneers at George Eliot? There is the kindred field of journalism, equally vast, into which she has hardly set foot, but in which her quick discernment, ready wit, fluent speech, and moral sensibility, peculiarly qualify her to succeed. There is the lecture platform. Twenty years ago, I own I felt a slight shrinking as I saw Grace Greenwood come upon the stage to read one of her beautiful lectures. Last week she addressed a large audience in Brooklyn. The élite of the city were there, and not an imp of the press whispered "indelicate." You may question Anna Dickinson's conclusions. You cannot deny her power, but you involuntarily say, "The tools to him who can use them." There is the pulpit, and the presence in it of those who remind us of the apostolic times, when "virgins did prophesy." The only Unitarian church in Connecticut is ably ministered unto by a woman; a female preacher acceptably fills the desk of the Universalist church in New Haven; and, within a year, I have heard the eloquent Quakeress, Miss Smiley, preach a very effective sermon from one of the leading Congregational pulpits of America. There is the medical profession, in which no one questions the propriety of an educated female physician prescribing for female patients and children. Especially, there is the work of school instruction. The prejudice, at one time very strong, against female teachers, is dying out. By the last census there are reported to be in the United States 221,000 instructors, of whom 127,000 are ladies. Not one of these teachers but would have been made more efficient by a higher education. Not one of their millions of pupils but would have felt the beneficent effects. A higher culture, more extensive attainments, loftier character, on the part of teachers—these are the one thing of which this nation is in greatest need. Skilled laborers of the highest type are scarce. Wooden-heads and wax-figures swarm. As Webster said of the legal profession, "It is crowded below, but there is plenty of room in the upper stories." Within three years, I have had applications from more than three hundred lady candidates desiring to teach, not one in fifty of whom could teach the higher English and classical studies. In these and in other departments of mental labor, there is room for educated women in larger numbers and of higher qualifications.

I know it will be answered that the appropriate sphere of woman is *home*. Be it so. There, too, she needs greater mental resources to save her from *ennui*, and its accompanying evils. "An idle head is the devil's workshop," for the manufacture of gossip, for fashion-worship, pleasure-hunting, dissipation, vice. Let her drink deep of the sweets of science and breathe freely the inspirations of literature, as a perpetual antidote to the tedium and the temptations of a home without children.

If she have children, still more will she need this thorough and exalted training. No task more difficult, more delicate, or more momentous, ever devolved upon a human being than falls to the lot of a mother in the rearing of her child to physical, mental, and moral perfection.

How precious the privilege, how rare yet how sublime the power, of conducting her own children, not through the steps of an elementary education merely, but through an academic or even a collegiate course! How many thousands of mothers throughout this land would find a lofty mission and perpetual blessedness in so teaching their aspiring children! How many tens of thousands of ingenuous youth, to whom fortune has denied the means of academic or collegiate education, might find in such instruction an unspeakable boon!

Young America is conceited, disrespectful, does not honor overmuch his mother. Commonly he soon outstrips, or thinks he outstrips, her mental attainments. Her stature dwindles as his increases. At best, in his fancied greatness, he pities while he loves her. But what if she has traversed every inch of these intellectual regions before him, has scaled those heights, has conquered those enemies, has looked deeper into those mysteries, is superior at every point, can in an instant flood his darkness with light, sweeps with steady gaze the circumference of his groping thought, and shows him ever an angelic intellect as well as a mother's heart! With such a mother, filial love would almost become worship.

Very eloquently and beautifully has one of the speakers, Professor Tyler, this afternoon spoken in his delightful way of that surpassing genius, in some respects perhaps the foremost intellect of modern times, Francis Bacon. How much of his greatness was due to his mother! She was the daughter of Sir Anthony Cooke, tutor to King Edward VI. Every evening when Sir Anthony came home, he taught his daughter the lessons he had given to his royal pupil. Anne Cooke mastered Latin, Greek, and Italian, and became eminent as a scholar and translator. She taught her son. A suggestion of Bacon's reverence for her, some conception of what he felt that he owed her, may be gained from the touching request in his will that he might be buried by her side. "For my burial, I desire it may be in St. Michael's Church at Gorhambury, for there is the grave of my mother."

Again, she needs education to fit her for the companionship of the educated. The vast disparity in mental stature between husband and wife has been a frequent cause of domestic infelicity. So Pericles and many an Athenian found it. The wicked and waggish old monk, who gave us the etymology of *celibate* and *celibacy*, *coeli beatitudo*, heaven's bliss, had doubtless seen the effect of this disparity in reversing the order of nature, the butterfly before marriage becoming the caterpillar after it, or, by a still more alarming metamorphosis, transformed into a hornet. Witness Socrates, Dante, Montaigne, Sir Thomas More, Shakespeare, Hooker, Molière, Milton, Rousseau, Dryden, Addison, Shelley.

But does not a collegiate education unfit her for home and household duties? Surely there is nothing in the nature of deep study or high thinking to make her less practical. Of Elizabeth Carter, whom Dr. Johnson pronounced the best Greek scholar in England, and who knew Hebrew, Greek, Latin, French, Italian, Spanish, and German, he said, "She can with equal skill make a pudding or translate Epictetus, work a handkerchief or compose a poem." Mrs. Browning's thorough acquaintance with Greek, Latin, and Hebrew, her profound studies and lofty genius, did not make her less admirable as a wife and mother. Mrs. Willard, in the home circle as in the company of *savans*, illustrated Wordsworth's "perfect woman, nobly planned."

After all, not matrimony but character, not widowhood nor motherhood, but moral and intellectual strength and beauty, is the great object of woman's existence. It is a common and most pernicious mistake to teach a girl that unwedded life is a failure. Happy she who can be, with Milton, "married to immortal verse," or can say, with Michael Angelo, "I have espoused my lot; my works shall be my children."

Finally, woman needs the higher education to rescue her from the possibility of becoming a noisy zealot. I take square issue with those idiotic youth and feeble-minded women of both sexes, with whom every learned woman is a "blue-stocking," and every "blue-stocking" is obtrusive, egotistical, immodest, boisterous—to sum up all in one bad word which ought to be a good word—"*strong-minded.*" The truth is precisely the reverse. Not education, but a lack of education; not high cultivation, but the absence of it, is the cause. Not the limiting, but the enlarging of the range of study, is the cure. It is only the superficially-educated that love to parade their intellectual power, or wag their loud sharp tongues. Increase of modesty comes with increase of knowledge.

Shallow draughts intoxicate the brain,
But drinking largely sobers us again."

Professor Silliman used to tell us that, from his second year in college, he had been generally estimating at a less figure his own achievements, until he had reached the humility of Newton, who saw all his discoveries as a few pebbles on a shoreless ocean. Glorious John Milton seldom errs; but he blunders sadly, when teaching his daughters to read but not to translate Latin; he justifies himself with the grim joke, "One tongue is enough for a woman." Von Moltke, the first of modern scientific warriors, before the splendor of whose military genius even the name of Napoleon grows pale, can speak in seven languages; ay, and "he can be silent in seven languages!"

But granting all that has been urged in behalf of advanced education for females, why coëducate?

Because young ladies should have the best possible advantages. No man honors more than I the munificence of Matthew Vassar, and those others who, with princely liberality, have endowed female colleges at Aurora, at Elmira, and elsewhere. But such institutions, without exception, are too limited in scope to afford the best opportunities to large numbers; too limited in curriculum of study, in apparatus, in library, in faculty, in equipments. It is not good policy to scatter resources and make two weak colleges, a college for the brothers, and another for the sisters, instead of one strong institution for both. Feeble colleges are better than none; but I submit that we have relatively too many of these—what shall I call them?—monohippic, uniequine, or, to use the homely vernacular, *one-horse* institutions. And we have not, nor are likely to have, a university exclusively for women.

Association with the other sex exerts such a refining influence, as nothing else can, upon each. Especially do young men need this. Many a scholar of profound erudition has made an utter failure in life, because of a lack of good manners and good breeding. Such instances will occur to every one, showing that the solitary student becomes either fatally timid, or fatally awkward, boorish, selfish. Neither in church, nor in school, nor in the family, is it good to be alone. A man can hardly be a complete gentleman, a woman can hardly be a complete lady, without the restraining, stimulating, and ennobling influence of the pure of the other sex.

Wherever earnest men and women are associated in the promotion of any good cause, such association is elevating and healthful. The testimony of colleges that coëducate to the good order and exemplary conduct of the students, is remarkable, and amply corroborates what I say, that association in this high work brings out what is manliest in young men, what is most womanly in young women.

Young people, like old people, are formed for society. Most of them will contrive to have it, under some circumstances or other. Hitherto their companionship has been almost wholly for pleasure, for display, for killing time, or for dissipation of some kind, in fashionable parties, in holiday excursions, in frolic, or small talk, or worse. Here, at least, they shall meet for serious, earnest, Christian work.

I have no fear of the results on female character. There exists, in some quarters, an unreasonable distrust of college students. As a body, even where they are at worst, I believe they will compare favorably in character with the average of young men in that community, and in many cases they are, as a class, superior. I know that the students of Cornell University, three years ago, were exceptionally correct in their bearing and conduct. For two years I was thrown into quite intimate relations with many of them, and never have met a class of young men that seemed to be of higher purposes, of purer motives, or more blameless deportment. There was a public sentiment among the students that would not tolerate anything dishonorable or mean. I know, too, the character of this Faculty and of the people of Ithaca. The moral atmosphere in which you all move is such, that I should esteem my son or daughter not unfortunate in coming within its influence.

But is there not danger that attachments will spring up? I take this bull by the horns, for it is a bull, worthy of Sir Boyle Roche himself. Yes, attachments will spring up; at least, I hope so. Under what conditions could they arise more favorably? In what circumstances could life-long companionships begin more auspiciously? How vastly are the chances for mistake in this important matter diminished by the wide range of intelligent selection! No, I do not fear these attachments. In those institutions where coëducation has been most thoroughly tried, I am informed that the unions so begun have been most happy; that they have not caused the fortunate subjects to swerve from the work of the class-room. "Love," says Landor, compressing a volume of wisdom into a sentence, "Love is a secondary passion with those that love most; a primary with those that love least." Ever honor and conscience control supremely those with whom love is most absorbing. Than such a love, really there is nothing nobler, nothing that more lifts in the scale of beings. Beautifully does Tennyson show its annihilation of selfishness:

> "Love took up the harp of life and smote on all the chords with might,
> Smote the chord of self, that, trembling, passed in music out of sight."

We can forgive Dick Steele a thousand slips and weaknesses, when we think of his more than chivalric ideal of womanhood, and that lofty utterance in regard to one whose saintly character and royal intellect had inspired him, "*to love her was a liberal education!*"

For these reasons I congratulate Mr. Sage on the auspicious work of which this day marks the beginning. God grant that his life may be spared to witness its consummation; to read the story of his beneficence in the grateful eyes of many hundreds of our fairest daughters; to see other universities and colleges following this good example, and flinging their gates wide open; to see, through many years, class after class go from these beautiful hills, laden with the choicest treasures of learning and science, to adorn thousands of Christian homes and enrich the common intellect of the nation; and to realize more and more, that each class is a successive wave of that incoming and outflowing tide, that is destined to rise higher and spread wider, till ignorance and crime shall vanish, and "the knowledge of the Lord shall cover the earth, as the waters cover the sea."

SPEECH OF DR. JAMES B. ANGELL, PRESIDENT OF THE UNIVERSITY OF MICHIGAN.

Mr. President, Ladies and Gentlemen:—I suppose few persons have traveled more hundreds of miles to be here to-day than I have; and I can think of few ocsions which would have called me from my duties, now unusually pressing, except this very one which places me before you at this hour.

The sight of this declining sun and of this patient company, already two hours and more upon their feet, would certainly incline me to embrace the opportunity which I asked for of your President, to sit quietly in my seat and rejoice with you at the benediction. But being upon my feet, I will say, if you have patience to wait and hear the simple words, that I am truly glad and proud to be able to stand here to-day. I am glad I can stand here, unworthy as I am to do it, to bring to you the greeting of the University and the State of of Michigan; for I think we have a right to rejoice with you here to-day. I think that I and my brethren of my old Faculty, whom I am sorry New York has stolen away from us, may claim it not only as our privilege, but also in some sense, if you will permit me to say so, as our right to sit with you here on this platform. We cannot but rejoice in the munificent generosity of your benefactor, who has laid the foundations of this structure so well; for his business interests in our State are so large that we regard him as almost a Michigan man; and when it is not known that he resides in New York, we claim him as a citizen of Michigan. We rejoice in this beautiful edifice as, in part, a Michigan gift. I rejoice, furthermore, in behalf of our University and our State, because your honored President here, as you all know, though Yale graduated him, won the first spurs of his intellectual knighthood under our roof—that knighthood which he has since illustrated so splendidly upon a hundred fields, and above all upon this now classic ground upon which we stand. It is not until after coming here to-day for the first time, and looking over this fair field crowned with these proud structures—it is not until now, that I have understood how he has been able to carry the weight of a responsibility almost too much for human strength to bear. It is because these harvests of beauty and glory have been springing up beneath his eye, even while the seed was falling from his hand. I come, too, to rejoice with you in the princely munificence of the Founder, who is known to us as to all men in the nation, and who never seemed nobler to me than since I have come to know, from striving to build up universities, what moral courage and self-denial it costs for a man in active business, like him, and Mr. Sage, and Mr. McGraw, to take clean out of their active business such sums as they have laid down here for you, and to say "*that* shall go for other men, not for me." We, my friends, you and I whom Providence has not trusted with the power to attempt this, we little know what the cost is, I fancy; and the older I grow and the more I see of men, the more do I look upon it as among the most heroic and courageous and noble of human acts. And above all, to my mind, is it hard for a man to retain his generosity and his confidence in his fellow men, enough to open his hand, when his motives are misconstrued at every step, and even the noblest deeds he does are turned into shafts with which to stab him to the heart. That is what calls for heroism and moral courage, to have confidence, to believe, and to keep doing good, certain that the day will come when man shall see, as God now sees, what the truth is.

It is, indeed, an auspicious beginning you have made to-day. I cannot but think that if there are any here who doubt at all the wisdom of this experiment, they must at least concede that this is a noble attempt to solve the problem which demands solution at the hands of American citizens—the problem, how to secure to women the same educational advantages long secured to man.

Notwithstanding all the wise words said here to-day, there is still a good deal of scepticism and doubt in the community, not about the duty of giving higher education to women, but about giving it in this particular way. Many would have it imparted by some other means, but ask by what means, and you do not readily get a satisfactory answer. Some say it is to be done by building up women's colleges; but pray who are to build them? Where are the Cornells and Sages, who will cover this land with colleges for women, as it is now filled with colleges for men? If women wait for that before securing their education, they go to their graves in ignorance. Concede, if you please, that colleges which have been already established for women are as meritorious as our colleges for men, which some will question, it still remains true that the number is so small, and must be so small for generations to come, that it cannot meet the demand. What then shall be done? The only other answer is of course the obvious one, to do what you are doing, and open the doors of colleges built for men.

So far as I have observed, the chief objections to this course group themselves under two or three heads. The first one, which used to be cited much more frequently than now, has been answered here so completely that I need but avert to it. It is this: that women are not capable of attaining to high culture. Well, my friends, that objection has been taken care of to-day. One would think from hearing these persons talk, that the young gentlemen who carry off the degrees of A. B. and B. P. had some marvelous attainments in literature and science. Well, we won't deny that among ourselves, undergraduates, but the men who have been through college are generally convinced that there is not so extraordinary an accumulation of knowledge in an ordinary college course, but that many a bright girl can get it, and now does get it. I give the result of the work at our University without any disparagement to the young men,—and I say in all frankness, that in all departments of study, the young ladies have fully held their own, to say the least, and no less in the higher mathematics than in the department of literature. They have shown the same variety of aptitude, the same variety of skill, that the young men have. Some have been brilliant, some have been less so, some have been broken at examination. That for your encouragement, young genmen, because we are impartial.

Another class of objections sum themselves up under this head—and to my mind it was formerly a much more formidable one, namely, that women have not the physical endurance to go through the course, and I do not doubt that mothers who hear me here to-day think so,—that it would be too heavy a draft upon the nervous strength of their daughters, and that they would break down and come home invalided. Now the only way this can be answered is of course by experiment. An American woman has said that any lady, who can endure the draft that modern dress and modern society make upon her, can certainly endure any college course so far as physical exhaustion is concerned. I am simply here to bear testimony, in the plainest way, to what our experience has shown. I have made it an object of particular examination and scrutiny, and I am thoroughly convinced that there is no danger which need be considered worthy of mention, in any young woman, in tolerably good health, pursuing the regular course prescribed, nor has it actually been the case that our young women have been impaired in health by the course.

The third class of objections, and the last I shall name, sum themselves up under this head: That there will be some kind of moral embarrassment which will be unpleasant, or that there will be some sacrifice of that peculiar charm, that delicacy which we describe by the term womanliness. None, certainly, can hold more firmly to this opinion than I, that if there were to be the slightest sacrifice of that charm, that delicacy which is to woman what color is to the flower, that nameless something that poets strive to describe but cannot, that something which attracts us to woman, and which in its essence charms as in all nature, if we may trust the German poet, who tells us, "*Das ewig Weibliche zieht us hinan,*" if this were to be lost, it were, indeed, in my judgment, too great a cost to pay. If we are to make masculine women, or blue stockings, then, for one, let me have the privilege of resigning my position. But I wish to testify, so far as my experience has gone,—I give it only as three years' experience,—I must say I see no tendency in this direction. We all know that American men, according to the testimony of Europeans, are proverbially courteous to ladies; and from students of colleges you may be assured you may rely upon courteous treatment toward ladies. So far as I know, though we have no regulations or rules in regard to the matter at all, but have left the whole thing to the innate good sense and courtesy of the students, I have yet to learn of the first thing which should cause the least apprehension upon this point. I speak with great plainness and emphasis, because I know this is a subject upon which there has been great concern, and upon which there was in my own mind at one time.

So much for these three points. I need not stop to argue upon them. The argument has been made by you and the verdict rendered. It is blooming up in stone before me, to stand for ages. I come to rejoice with you—not so much to argue with you—but to rejoice with you in the bright auguries of this day. Why, my friends, there is no such thing as jealousy between good colleges, and good universities. Depend upon it, it is only a poor college that is jealous of a good one. It is only a mean man who is envious of a worthy one. If you hear backbiting conversation by a man, you can form your opinion of *him*, whatever you may think of the man he is talking about; and that is true of colleges. No, my friends, you cannot make this college so splendid that we shall not rejoice in it, cannot win a success here that we shall not rejoice in. Every good college helps every other good college, and every good man helps every other good man on the face of the earth. This is the true spirit, and I come here to ask you to lock shields in this good work, and to move on in the advance in this noble work, in the common battle against ignorance and prejudice. That is what these American colleges mean, and I thank God for the success which has crowned you here. As I stand here and look around me to-day, remembering that only six years ago there was nothing here, I fairly rub my eyes and ask if this is not some dream of the Arabian Nights. It is like the stones of the castle which grew up in a night with splendid minaret and turret. I rejoice with you to-day. My University rejoices with you to-day. The State of Michigan rejoices with you to-day. Let us go on, my friends, now and always doing the best work we can for this and every institution of learning throughout the land. That is our high vocation, and you young gentleman, and you young ladies, who are coming here, have your part in it as truly as we have. That is the message which I bring to you—missionary if you please from the western prairies, as the President has intimated,—that you may always proceed upon the same mission wherever you may go, conveying good news and glad tidings to the studious youth of this land.

The exercises closed with the Lord's prayer pronounced by Dr. Wilson, and the benediction.

DESCRIPTION OF THE BUILDING.

The Sage College is arranged in the form of a quadrangle. The front portion of the building is four stories in height, and contains on the first floor a parlor, reception-room, matron's rooms, class-room, and several students'-rooms; and on the other floors, a library, teacher's parlor, music rooms, infirmary, and dormitories. The south wing gives accomodations for the botanical department of the University, a lecture-room analyzing-room, professor's study, and museum. In the north wing are the dining-room, kitchen, laundry, bakery, pantries, store-rooms and servants' rooms. The upper stories are arranged as dormitories or students' rooms. The eastern portion is the gymnasium. There are accommodations for one hundred and twenty students, besides officers, teachers and servants. There are five stair-cases, so arranged that in case of fire in any part of the building, every occupant can escape by some one of them. Water and gas-pipes are to be laid throughout the whole establishment. Ample provision is made for ventilation by means of four large shafts, artificially heated. The building is to be warmed by steam. The appointments in the way of bath-rooms, water-closets, ranges, laundry fixtures, etc., will be complete and of the most approved description. The foundations are of stone, and the walls above them of red brick, with dressings of New Jersey brown stone and bands and arches of black and yellow bricks. Behind the south wing a large conservatory is to be built, connected with the botanical department. The entire cost of the buildings when completed and furnished will be $150,000.

REPORT

SUBMITTED TO THE TRUSTEES OF CORNELL UNIVERSITY, IN BEHALF OF A MAJORITY OF THE COMMITTEE ON MR. SAGE'S PROPOSAL TO ENDOW A COLLEGE FOR WOMEN.

By ANDREW D. WHITE, Chairman of the Committee.

Albany, February 13, 1872.

REPORT.

TO THE BOARD OF TRUSTEES OF THE CORNELL UNIVERSITY:—

Gentlemen:—The Committee appointed at your last meeting to examine and report concerning the establishment of an institution for the education of women in connection with the University, as well as in regard to any proffer of an endowment for that purpose, respectfully submit the following

REPORT.

Your Committee began at once an extended correspondence with persons in various parts of the country, whose experience, in the education of the sexes together, gives their statements value; they also obtained various documents bearing on the question.

But in this correspondence they did not consult the authorities of colleges which had never tried the system. They had before them, already, a long report based on information thus obtained—the report made to the Regents of the University of Michigan several years since—when the subject was first broached in that State. The Regents' committee wrote to a large number of eminent gentlemen connected with the venerable institutions of learning in the older States, and to a very small number of others. The result was what might have been expected. It was as if the Japanese authorities, aroused to the necessity of railroads and telegraphs, had corresponded with eminent Chinese philosophers regarding the ethics of the subject, instead of sending persons to observe the working of railroads and telegraphs where they are already in use. Of course, the great majority of responses to that committee were overwhelmingly against the admission of women. It was declared to be "contrary to nature," "likely to produce confusion," "dangerous," "at variance with the ordinances of God;" in short, every argument that a mandarin would be sure to evolve from his interior consciousness against a railroad or a telegraph which he had never seen, these correspondents reproduced against a system of education they had never tried.

Nor did your Committee think it just to give theories on one side, without giving them as fully on the other. Against the theories of the eminent men referred to, it would be only fair to set those of such men as John Stuart Mill and Henry Thomas Buckle. Such a discussion would have made the report very cumbrous, and it has been judged best to present, mainly, facts and reasoning based on the experiences of those who by practice know something of the matter.

A subordinate Committee, consisting of Messrs. Sage and White, was therefore appointed to visit leading universities and colleges to which young women had been admitted with young men, and to make examination into their various systems, and their results, moral and intellectual.

The institutions visited were Oberlin College, the State University of Michigan, the Northwestern University, near Chicago, the State Industrial University of Illinois, and Antioch College, at Yellow Springs, Ohio, the college in whose work that noble citizen, Horace Mann, gave up his life. The State University of Wisconsin had been previously visited by a member of the Committee; the State Agricultural College of Iowa presented an example too recent to carry great weight; but a valuable letter was received from its President, discussing the subject and stating facts established in a long previous experience.

It was with some surprise that the Committee,—even those members whose attention had been long directed to the subject,—found how great a body of facts had already been established, tending to the solution of the question in hand.

That there had been much presentation of *theories* on one side and the other, they well knew. Discussions as to woman's mental and moral capacity, her sphere of activity, her equality with man or subordination to him,—theories, physiological, psychological, political, æsthetical and biblical, they were aware, had been presented in endless variety; but they now learned more clearly than ever before that, in this matter, there is a vast body of *facts*,—the outgrowth of various ideas, upon various soils, in accordance with various systems, under various degrees of freedom.

It seemed their first duty to investigate these facts separately, then to collate them, then to throw any light thus concentrated into various theories and programmes.

First of all, it was found that, for very many years,—in fact during the greater part of the century,—the education together of young men and young women of marriageable age, and coming from distant homes, had been going on all about us, in the academies and high schools of the State of New York and neighboring States, and that not only have no evil results followed worthy to be taken into the account, but the system has worked so well that it has come to be regarded as natural and normal.

While this practical experiment has thus been going on for many years, under almost perfect freedom as regards boarding, lodging and social intercourse, with no well-watched quadrangles, no system of proctors to restrain the young men, or of matrons to guard the young women, the disputants on this question, on either side, appear to have been straining their eyes in looking deep down into the human consciousness or afar off into the universe at large, to solve a problem which their fathers and mothers, and sons and daughters had done so much already to work out,—nay, in whose solution they themselves had taken part.

Among the letters giving results obtained in this field of experience, none certainly is entitled to greater weight than that of the Honorable Samuel B. Woolworth, for thirty-two years the successful principal of some of the best academies in the State, and of one which, under his management, ranked in many respects the first. It should be added that this direct personal experience of Dr. Woolworth is supplemented by an experience of many years as Secretary of the Board of Regents of the State of New York—a position bringing him into most intimate relations with every academy and high school in the State. His letter is as follows:—

"All my experience in teaching has been in institutions to which persons of both sexes have been admitted—at Onondaga Academy six years—at Cortland Academy twenty-two years—at the State Normal School four years.

"I answer your questions *seriatim*:—

"1. The coëducation of the sexes has been favorable to good order and discipline.

"2. A mutual stimulating influence has been exerted on scholarship.

"3. There have been no scandals—at least not more than may exist between the members of a school limited to one sex, and the outside world.

"4. To most of the academies, and to all of the normal and union schools of the State, both sexes are admitted."

The letters received from the Principals of the State

Normal Schools bear similar testimony. The Reverend Joseph Alden, D. D., writes of his five years' experience in the education of young men and young women together as Principal of the State Normal School at Albany, that "no evil has been experienced here;" but that after an experience of thirty-five years as student, tutor, professor, and president, in six different colleges, his "opinion is *fixed* on the subject that ladies should not be admitted to *our colleges*."

Doctor Alden gives no facts nor arguments in support of this position, stating that "the grounds of this opinion, if committed to writing, would cover more space than your Committee would care to go over; and I presume that my views of college education differ so materially from theirs, as to render my own premises unsound in their view."

The Doctor concludes by saying of his Normal School experience, that he "don't think that it proves anything with reference to a college."

It is to be regretted that the Doctor does not give the Committee the benefit of the facts and reasonings that have brought him to this conclusion.

It will however be observed by a reference to the letter as given in the appendix, that in neither of the colleges with which he had been connected had the experiment of coëducation of the sexes been tried; and while the Committee are ready to give full weight to any expression of opinion by one so justly respected, even though unsupported by any actual experience, and at variance with his acknowleged experience in the State Normal School, they think that it should be very carefully compared with that of the other Principals of Normal Schools in the State.

But before giving their testimony, which is without exception favorable to coëducation, a point should be specially noted in regard to the analogy between the instruction in the State Normal Schools and the colleges. Dr. Alden asserts his belief that this analogy is too remote to form the basis for a sound inference in favor of admitting young women to college.

In the absence of any arguments or presentation of facts by the Doctor to support this statement of opinion, the Committee are left to their own unaided reason on the subject, and they can only say that argument from successful coëducation in normal schools to successful coëducation in colleges and universities, seems to them logically irresistible. In both cases the students are of marriageable age, and from distant homes,—in both cases great freedom is allowed, though in this matter the argument is, *a fortiori*, for success in education in the colleges, rather than in the normal schools, for the colleges generally have dormitories under some little control, while the normal schools generally have none. Besides this, if there is any force in the argument so often urged in favor of classical education, that it gives refinement and higher culture, still stronger is the argument in favor of successful coëducation in colleges, rather than normal schools.

From the testimony of the other principals the following extracts present fair examples.

Principal Sheldon, of the State Normal School at Oswego, writes of coëducation:—"I think the influence is good on both sexes, socially, morally, and intellectually. My experience in all grades of schools below the university has confirmed me in this opinion. This experience has led me to feel that it would work equally well in the university. Of this, however, I cannot be so confident, as the conditions here are somewhat changed. I am now making a practical experiment in this direction by sending my own daughter to Michigan University."

Principal J. W. Armstrong, D. D., of the State Normal School at Fredonia, writes:—"My observation shows that the morals of students of either sex deteriorate, apparently, in proportion to the rigor of the separation of the sexes. The same is true of their delicacy of feeling, their sense of honor, and their love of truth.

"In all mixed seminaries and academies where social intercourse of the sexes was either forbidden or largely restrained, the ladies lost in prudence, delicacy, and truthfulness, even faster than the gentlemen.

"For many years my views of school government have been more liberal than the common practice would justify. In this Normal School I allow, and *even encourage*, all the freedom of intercourse between the sexes, which would be allowed in a well-regulated family. This has been tested for two years. The results are good in the recitation-room, where they mingle as they choose on the seats; in the halls, where they communicate freely as at home; in the boarding-places, where they have only the same restrictions. They visit, walk, and ride out together, out of recitation hours, whenever and wherever they please. The results are, they study better, are more polite, *visit far less, walk and ride together far less*, than when restrained, and *never under imprudent or objectionable circumstances.*

"We have the most orderly, studious, and happy school I ever was in.

"In Genesee College the results were good, though the restrictions were too many to allow the best results.

"All my experience and observations have confirmed my earlier faith in the sense and virtues of the youth of the land who attend our schools, of the necessity of the two sexes exerting reciprocally their influence upon their development, in order to obtain the best results, and of the fact that nine-tenths of all the irregularity and disorder in our colleges arises from the establishment of an arbitrary and unnatural state of society among the students.

"I have written you in great haste and candidly."

It will be seen that Dr. Armstrong's experience extends both to colleges and normal schools, and that while arriving at an opposite conclusion from that reached by Dr. Alden, he does not hesitate to support it both by facts and arguments.

Says Principal Hoose, of the State Normal School at Cortland:—

" My immediate personal observation and experience cover about eight or ten years of college life where both sexes recited together and attended college upon an equality of privileges.

" I saw no harm, but good results; scholarship was as good, conduct better in regard to roughness, etc., than when the sexes were separated.

" My opinion, based upon general experience, observation, and principles, is in favor of the admission, etc."

Prof. J. W. Dickinson, of the State Normal School at Westfield, Mass., says :—

" There is always a state of uneasiness among boys and girls when they are collected apart from one another. This is clearly seen in our colleges and young ladies' seminaries. The presence of young ladies exerts a restraining and refining influence over young men, and the presence of young men exerts an influence that tends to give strength and dignity to the characters of young ladies. We have had no trouble arising from the association of the two sexes in our school."

From these statements, from an overwhelming body of other testimony, and from what may be observed all about us in nearly every town in the State, it will be seen that the successful education of youth of both sexes—of marriageable age—coming from distant homes, left to themselves almost entirely as to their choice of homes and associates, guided by their own judgment as to social intercourse and general conduct, is a *fact*, a fact not confined to recent experience, not restricted to a narrow territory, but a fact of many years standing, a fact established in nearly every county of this and neighboring States.

It may, however, still be claimed that there is no analogy between instruction in academies, high schools and normal schools, and instruction in universities and colleges; or in other words, that human nature in persons studying algebra, geometry, languages, and natural, moral and mental philosophy, in an institution called an academy or normal school, is not the same as in persons of the same age pursuing the same general lines of study, in an institution called a college or university.

The simple statement of the proposition would seem to carry its own refutation; but let it be conceded. The Committee pass to the facts established in the colleges and universities themselves.

The system of educating young men and young women together in colleges and universities is very much more recent than their coëducation in academies and high schools.

The causes are not difficult to find; one is simple matter of history. The colleges of this country inherited a semi-monastic system from those of the mother country. Those of the mother country inherited many controlling ideas of their system from times before the Reformation, when universities were almost entirely in the hands of a clergy vowed to celibacy.

6

The colleges and universities have been far less amenable to public opinion than academies and high schools have been, the latter being controlled by men taken from the communities in which the schools were situated, and representing the average common sense of those communities; the former more by faculties, bred mainly in the traditional ideas, and by trustees, too remote to feel warranted in making radical changes. Under such a system, mandarinism is almost inevitable. The traditional studies, the traditional modes of government, the traditional habits of thought will naturally be regarded as the only sound and safe; they will be argued for and fought for, to the last, by every graduate honored with a degree, and every mandarin glorified with a button.

Still, justice must be done the older colleges, by saying that some of their greatest men have been hopeful as to the education of both sexes together.

In the letter of President Mark Hopkins, of Williams College, to the Committee of Regents of the University of Michigan, written in 1858, occurs the following passage:—

"The question you put me is one of no little interest. * * * There are difficulties and embarassments connected with it, still my impression is that the advantages connected with our higher institutions for young men, might be shared by young women to a great extent, with great advantage to both. Probably the course of study should not be the same throughout, but in many things there certainly could be no objections to the continuance of that association in study, which is begun at the common school; and there would be many advantages from it. The difficulty would be social; if intercourse of the classes and aside from study could be properly regulated, it would work well. That would depend much on the arrangements you might be able to make, and on the tone of sentiment in the community. * * * My impression is that you might try the experiment safely, and I hope you will do so."

A letter from the venerable President Nott, of Union College, to the same Committee, at the same period, dwells on the wide prevalence of the theory, that difference of sex necessitates separation in education, on the difficulties and dangers, on fears "that what is gained to manners by diminished rudeness in one sex, would be more than counterbalanced by loss of native modesty in the other." In another letter, written to the trustees, he says:—"I would like to see the experiment tried under proper regulations, * * * and were I at the head of a university in Michigan, and public opinion called for the trial of the experiment, I should not oppose obedience to the call. Corporations are always conservative; it is their nature not to lead, but to follow public opinion, and often far in the rear. That it will not be approved by college corporations generally, may be taken for granted."

This latter prediction, the correspondence of the Board of Regents proved true. An overwhelming opposition is shown by the letters from the authorities of nearly all the older colleges.

It was thought by the writers that the results would be "demoralizing;" that "young men would lose a proper sense of the dignity of their own pursuits;" that the results would be "degradation" and "corruption;" that "it would deprive both sexes of the cultivation peculiar to each;" that "the delicacy of female character would be destroyed;" that "common morality would suffer;" that "it would tend to unwoman woman;" that "the success of the measure would produce confusion;" that "to confound the higher education of the two sexes, would lead to lamentable consequences;" that "the effects of such a system would probably be to give them false ideas of life in general and of their particular spheres, than which nothing could be more injurious in the forming stage of character;" that "a present and local popularity might be gained, but at a fearful ultimate expense and the disapprobation of men of science and learning throughout the country."

These statements of theory have an interest; but as they are confessedly not based on observation, they seem to your Committee to be entitled to the same weight, and no more, that is given the testimony of theorists on the opposite side who seem to suppose that all evil is to be banished, all passion subdued, and a millenium of pure thoughts and good manners immediately brought in by a breaking down of the barriers which now divide the sexes in advanced education.

From these statements of theories we turn to recitals of facts.

The first college visited by the Committee, was Oberlin College, Ohio. There were found a very large number of students of both sexes. For the young men, dormitories were provided on the usual plan; for the young women, a large and well-appointed building with matron and assistants, but the increasing numbers of students have obliged the college authorities to allow both young men and women to board in families in the town; the same cause has also led the authorities to admit young men in large numbers to the privileges of the dining hall. Your Committee dined in the college hall with two hundred students, about half of whom were young men, and half young women. The order was excellent,—the appearance of all neat and cleanly. The young men and young women sat at the same table, on opposite sides; the conversation was quiet; there was, throughout, an air of refinement which the member of the Committee more familiar with college life has never seen at a table frequented by men alone.

In the recitation rooms a similar result was observed. They seemed decidedly more orderly than those in which young men are educated by themselves. Recitations were attended in different branches of mathematics, and in ancient and modern languages. The young ladies, while showing self-possession, appeared refined, quiet and modest. Their exercises were in all cases performed as well as those of the young men, in many cases better.

The Committe visited the students in their rooms to

get at their ideas; they also talked with citizens of the town. The general statement was that the results had been good,—that the evil results, so generally prophesied, had not been seen,—that the system appeared to work well.

In the light of his experience, the President of the institution, the Reverend Dr. Fairchild, states that "the proportion of young ladies has not for many years fallen below one-third, nor risen above one-half, except during the war, when the ladies predominated in the ratio of five to four;" that the present number of students is about one thousand, but that the greater part of these are in what ought to be called a preparatory department; that in the college course proper, the proportion of ladies to gentlemen has risen as high as one to four, but that it now stands as one to ten; that the boarding-halls having been found insufficient, students have been allowed to board in families; that "the special discipline of young ladies is committed to the Lady Principal, assisted by a ladies' board of managers composed in general of wives of professors in the college. The advice of the College Faculty is sometimes taken, but the young ladies do not come before them for discipline."

There are no monitors, "but each one makes a weekly report of success or failure in the performance of prescribed duties. Young ladies boarding in families have their reports countersigned by the matron of the house, who is, in a degree, responsible for the conduct of her charge."

The association of the young men and women outside of the class-room is regulated as experience seems to require; some provision is made for social intercourse, visiting is allowed under rules dictated by common sense.

A very useful element in the preservation of proper relations between the two sexes is found in the presence of brothers and sisters, who are of course mutually sensitive as to any thing that would tend to degrade each other.

The social culture is found valuable. "To secure this, the student does not need to make any expenditrure of time, going out of his way or leaving his proper work, for the pleasure or improvement resulting from society. He finds himself naturally in the midst of it, and he adjusts himself to it instinctively. It influences his manners, his feelings, his thoughts. He may be as little conscious of the sources of the influence as of the sunlight or the atmosphere; it will envelope him all the same, saving him from the excessive introversion, the morbid fancies, the moroseness which sometimes arise in secluded study,—giving elasticity of spirits and even of movement, and refinement of character not readily attained out of society. It seems desirable that our young men especially should enjoy these advantages during the period of their courses of study, while the forces that form character work most effectually."

It is also declared that good order is greatly promoted. There have been no difficulties in the college dining-hall.

"There has been an entire absence of the irregularities and roughness, so often complained of in college."

The Committee cannot but consider this as a crucial test. The Oberlin College table is probably the only one on the continent of which this can be said.

The system promotes morality. "Evils that might be tolerated in the shape of drinking saloons and other places of dissipation, if young men only were present, seem intolerable when ladies are gathered with them."

As to ability to maintain an excellent standing in college classes, Doctor Fairchild declares that during his own experience as professor—eight years in ancient languages, Latin, Greek, and Hebrew,— eleven in mathematics, abstract and applied,—and eight in philosophical and ethical studies—he has never observed any difference in the sexes as to performance in the recitations. He is careful to state, however, that he does not at all believe or consider that it follows from the above that there are not great differences in mental and moral characteristics between man and woman, fatal to the theories of those known as "strong-minded women."

As to health it seems best to give his own words :—

"Nor is there any manifest inability on the part of young women to endure the required labor. A breaking down in health does not appear to be more frequent than with young men. We have not observed a more frequent interruption of study on this account ; nor do our statistics show a greater draft upon the vital forces in the case of those who have completed the full college course. Out of eighty-four young ladies who have graduated since 1841, seven have died—a proportion of one in twelve. Of three hundred and sixty-eight young men who have graduated since that date, thirty-four are dead, or a little more than one in eleven. Of these thirty-four young men, six fell in the war, and, leaving these out, the proportion of deaths still remains one to thirteen. Taking the whole number of gentlemen graduates, omitting the theological department, we find the proportion of deaths one to nine and a half; of ladies, one to twelve; and this, in spite of the lower average expectation of life for women, as indicated in life insurance tables. The field is, of course, too narrow for perfectly conclusive results; but there is no occasion for special apprehension of failure of health to ladies from study."

The Doctor also alludes to the fear so often felt that under this system "the young men will become frivolous and effeminate, and the young women coarse and masculine." As regards men, he says:—"We have found it the surest way to make men of boys, and gentlemen of rowdies." As to the young women, he says:—"You would know whether the result with us has been a large accession of coarse, 'strong-minded' women, in the offensive sense of the word; and I say without hesitation, that I do not know of a single instance of such a product as the result of our system of education."

To show that the system of joint education "does not bewilder woman with a vain ambition or tend to turn her aside from the work which God has impressed upon her entire constitution"—that is, the duties of a wife and mother, it is stated that "of the eighty-four ladies who have taken the college course, twenty-seven only are unmarried, and, of these, four died early, and of the remaining twenty-three, twenty are graduates of less than six years standing."

In answer to the question whether young people will, under such a system, form such acquaintances as will result, during their course of study or after they leave college, in matrimonial engagements, the Doctor says:—"Undoubtedly they will, and if this is a fatal objection, the system must be pronounced a failure. The majority of young people form such acquaintances between the ages of sixteen and twenty-four, and these are the years devoted to a course of study. It would be a most unnatural state of things if such acquaintances should not be made."

He then says very pertinently:—"The reasonable inquiry in the case is whether such aquaintances and engagements can be made under circumstances more favorable to a wise and considerate adjustment or more promising of a happy result."

Finally the subject of immoralities and scandals is taken up. The Doctor is understood to assert that sporadic cases of scandal may occur, as has happened in the most carefully guarded seminaries under the old system, and even in monastic institutions, but that this is all that is to be feared.

The address from which the extracts are made, closes with the following words:—

"'In concluding this statement, permit me to say that I have no special call as an apostle or propagandist of this system of education. The opinions set forth are such as with my limited experience I am compelled to cherish, and when called upon, as now, I cheerfully express them."

The Committee feel bound to add that these words seem in accordance, not only with the entire spirit of the report itself, but also with all the facts obtained by them at Oberlin.

The Committe next visited the State University of Michigan. Here young women were admitted about four years since. The system is the opposite of that at Oberlin. There is no preparatory department, there is no building set apart for the young women, they are left free to choose their own boarding-houses and form their own associations as they see fit. During the first year after young women were admitted, there was but one who availed herself of the privilege; there are now sixty, and this number is about equally divided between the Colleges of Literature, Science and Arts on the one side, and the Colleges of Law and Medicine on the other. Young men and women attend lectures and recitations together, except in the Medical College, where separate courses are provided.

The general testimony was in favor of the new order of things. Some individuals in the faculty and many citizens whose opinions are entitled to respect, still declared themselves disbelievers in the system;

but their position was based upon general principles and no fact was adduced in support of it.

On the other hand the sub-committee found that the leading mathematician in one of the classes, who had carried off a prize over the whole class, for solving a difficult problem which had been presented, without finding a solution for several years, was a young woman. They were also reminded that one of the best Greek scholars in the institution for many years, was a young woman; and the class exercises generally showed that the young women were not at all behind the young men. There was also obtained from the Professor of Natural History, Dr. Winchell, a very ingenious and careful table of statistics regarding the study of botany.

This table, which is appended to the report, aims to show the relative proficiency of young men and women; and then, without regard to sex, of students in the classical course, students in the course where Latin is studied, but not Greek, students in the scientific course, and some others. The results were obtained by a careful award of marks in a given scale, upon a written examination held in June, 1871.

The points on which the comparison was made were two, viz:—The subject of botany itself, and style in writing, etc. In the comparison as regards botany itself, "all young women" stood first on the whole list; all young men stood eleventh. In the comparison as regards style, etc., "all young women" stood first, and "all young men" seventh. The average standing in botany on a scale of 100 was 93 for the young women, against 70 for the young men. In orthography the mean number of words misspelled by the young women was 1.91, and by the young men 4.95. The proportional number of words misspelled was for the young women 22, for the young men 56. In every respect the young women gained the victory.

The Committee also heard in the class-rooms recitations in the languages by young women, showing as much clearness and vigor as those by young men.

They conversed with some of the young lady students and were most favorably impressed by their quiet dignity, modesty and refinement. The testimony of these, as regards danger to health from collegiate study, was, that though there had been occasional cases of injury from overwork, the general health of young women in college is quite as good as that of young women out of college.

As to trouble arising from the mingling of the two sexes in the university town, there has been less social intercourse between the young women and young men, than between the latter and the daughters of citizens in the town, not in college; the young ladies seem to be quietly on their guard against receiving too much attention from students of the other sex.

As to order, Professor Frieze, formerly the honored acting President of the institution, than whom no one could be more careful and conscientious in a statement of the kind, writes:—"One fact may be of interest. The janitor of the recitation building, who has been in service four or five years, has repeatedly said, and still says, that the conduct of students in that building in moving from room to room, and especially in passing up and down the staircases, is very greatly improved. They are almost free from crowding, shouting, etc.,—the old complaints. He is sure this increased gentleness in manners is due to the presence of the ladies; having noticed frequently the effect of their presence in the halls."

One of the members of your Committee, during the visit to that University, was under circumstances very favorable to the formation of a correct judgment on this point. For five years, during the period before the admission of young women, he was in daily familiar intercourse with the students of the institution as a professor. He can hardly be mistaken in the belief that there has taken place a decided change for the better, as regards student manners in the recitation rooms, and in personal neatness and tidiness.

As to the general effect, Professor Cooley, of the Law Department, Chief Justice of the State, and a resident near the university grounds, writes:—

"The admission of women has scarcely caused a ripple on the surface of university matters. * * * From the moment the thing became an accomplished fact, it has been to every one here a matter, I may almost say, of entire indifference. As yet I have witnessed no evil results whatever. You are misinformed if you are told that the standard of admission is lowered; the tendency has been in the other direction."

Other valuable letters might be given, from members of the Michigan University Faculty, but these are selected because the well-known judicial fairness of the writers, places them beyond cavil.

Tha University of Michigan should not be dismissed before alluding to one more point of great importance. The general testimony was, that the young lady students were more *conscientious* in study than the young men, and that this was the main cause of their remarkable success in every class and study.

The next visit was made to the North Western University, at Evanston, near Chicago, an institution largely endowed, and under control of the Methodist Episcopal Church. Here the ladies' hall was visited, and the experience of the President and several members both of the governing and instructing bodies obtained.

The experiment did not seem to have been so fully tried as at the establishments previously visited; but the universal testimony was in its favor.

Meeting the instructors and lady students, socially in their hall, and setting with them at their table, it was evident that the last charge in the world which any sane man could think of bringing against them, would be lack of feminine dignity, refinement, modesty or delicacy.

The next visit was to the Illinois Industrial University, at Champaign, Illinois, about one hundred and thirty miles south of Chicago. This is one of the recipients of the United States land grant, and is progressing in a manner most satisfactory, under the presidency of the Honorable John M. Gregory, formerly the very successful Superintendent of Public Instruction in the State of Michigan.

The same absence of the evil results so long predicted by theorists, the same good found elsewhere, under the system of joint education, was found here. Many interesting facts regarding this institution have to be omitted for lack of time.

The final visit of the series was to Antioch College, at Yellow Springs, Ohio, the institution noted as the place where the final work of Horace Mann was accomplished.

Here a system is established more akin to the restrictive system at Oberlin, than the free system of the University of Michigan; there are separate halls for the two sexes, and the young ladies' hall is kept under careful supervision.

Visits to the recitation rooms showed that the young women were quite equal to the young men as regards native ability and conscientious study.

In the dining hall both sexes were found together, as at Oberlin, and the code of dining-table ethics was evidently superior to that which generally exists when a great body of young men take their meals by themselves. Nothing could be better of its kind than the bearing of the young women. Here, too, there was an utter lack of those masculine or semi-masculine characteristics, that want of refinement and feminine modesty which has been predicted by the theorists.

A written statement to the Committee by the present President, the Reverend G. W. Hosmer, D. D., contains much information of interest.

He says:—" I have been president of this college for five years. Of the one hundred and seventy students—about the average number in attendance in all departments—one-third have been women, and the average age of all our students has been twenty years, nearly. In this institution both sexes have been received from the beginning with Horace Mann, eighteen years ago.

" My personal knowledge for five years, and what I have known of the institution from its beginning, make me say confidently that the experiment has been successful.

" You ask for my opinion as to the effect of coëducation upon the intellectual progress, and upon the character and conduct of the young men, and also upon the progress, character and conduct of the young women.

" I think the young men have not been hindered, but rather quickened and urged forward in study; and as to character and conduct, I am sure they have been improved; rendered more orderly, gentle, and manly; and I think the young women have studied with more earnest and stronger purpose, and with us, I am sure their character has not suffered, but rather in character and conduct they have been benefited. On the whole, I think our young men have been made more gentle, and our young women stronger and more earnest, by being members of the same institution, and meeting in the recitations.

"You ask me next, if, on the whole, I think the coëducational plan is advantageous to the community, or otherwise. I consider that better, more thorough education of women is vital to the welfare of society, and I think that the coëducation plan, with a large elective privilege in taking studies, is a sure way to such better and thorough education.

"Lastly, you ask me if it be better to have separate lodging-houses and rules to regulate the conduct of the young men and women; or to leave them to their own sense of right and of propriety.

"We have a separate building for the young women, and a matron who lives with them, making family life as nearly as can be; and we have rules to prevent indiscretion, so that I think that it is true that our young people, while they enjoy in a large measure the intercourse of home life, are held from dangers more securely than they could be in the usual order of American society.

"I asked Horace Mann, the year he died, if he regarded his experiment of coëducation a success: 'Yes,' he said, 'but the success has been more by a care and vigilance brought as near to omniscient supervision, as it is possible for man to bring them.'

"We too, have been careful, but not *severely scrutinizing*, and I think that our young people enjoy their student life more than is common in colleges. Our institution is more like a home than any institution can be, in which one sex is admitted.

"In a city where the young men and women could live widely separated in the homes, and only come together in the recitations, there might be no need of many regulations, but if the institution be in a town or village, I should think there must be separate halls for the young men and young women, and judicious regulations, and a parental watchfulness."

The Agricultural College of Iowa was not visited, but the following letter from its president, the Honorable A. S. Welch, formerly principal of the State Normal School of Michigan, and for a time Senator of the United States from the State of Florida, seems especially valuable.

"I have had charge of two State institutions, to both of which young men and young women are admitted. One of them is, as you may remember, the State Normal School of Michigan, the other, this college, which was opened in the spring of '69. Michigan Normal School comprised about two hundred young women and fifty young men, all of whom found board in the different families of the city.*

"In this institution we have about fifty young women and one hundred and fifty young men, most of whom board in the same hall, the ladies having rooms in the wing of the same building.

"The executive charge of these two institutions has given me sixteen years of observation and experience in the coëducation of the sexes, and I am *unqualifiedly* in favor of it.

* Ypsilanti, a town with about half the population of Ithaca.

" First, I am sure that the effect of the system on the intellectual progress and on the conduct and character of both the young men and the young women, is, *in every well regulated institution*, safe and salutary.

" Second, all the results I have reached warrant the belief that the collegiate education of young men and young women in the same classes, *is* advantageous to the community. Apart from the experience I have had, I do not see how the isolation of one sex from the other during the period given to the higher education, can secure a better scholarship, or more refinement of manners or greater purity of morals.

" Of course there will be trouble in the government of colleges which admit both sexes, but such troubles will, I believe, be less serious and more easily managed than the rougher ones incident to colleges conducted on the plan of sexual isolation.

" If young ladies attending college find their homes with the better families of the city, their intercourse with the young men may be left largely to their own judgment and to the influences which such families will naturally have over them, but if circumstances compel you to gather them into a boarding-hall, they should, it seems to me, be put under the immediate supervision of a competent matron, and their social intercourse with the young men be limited to certain hours. They will help, rather than hinder the good order of the recitation room."

It seems now advisable to find what light may be thrown upon the subject of our investigation by a collation of the various facts obtained, and of the reasonings to which those facts have given rise; and first, as to its effects on the present body of students.

EFFECTS ON YOUNG MEN.

As to the effect on character and manners, there seems no exception to the rule that the admission of young women to colleges and universities, thus far, has tended to refine the young men; from the declarations of such men as Presidents Fairchild, Hosmer and Armstrong, down to the plain statement of facts by the janitor of the University of Michigan, the testimony on this point is concurrent.

The question may be asked, "Is this a healthful refinement?" It would appear to be so. It is just what is sought for young men in the world at large. Nothing is more universally acknowledged to be a blessing to young men in society, than association with young women whose thoughts and pursuits are of an ennobling kind. That the women entering a university will be of this class, is in the nature of things. No frivolous young woman, no mere petted and spoiled beauty of a season, will be likely to wish to undergo the moral restraint or mental labor demanded in such a course, and if such an one were to enter from caprice, she would be certain to depart soon. It was once said with authority, of a noble and educated woman, "To know her was a liberal education," and within a month, one of the most noted divines and thinkers in this country, a man not at all an advocate of what are known as "woman's rights," has stood up and declared his very great indebtedness to two women of noble gifts of heart and mind.*

But will this refinement be gained at the cost of manly qualities? As to this we might balance theory against theory. If it be argued, *a priori*, on the one hand, that much association with young women is likely to make young men take on some unmanly qualities, it can be just as strongly argued on the other, that the association is likely, while increasing refinement, to bring out the distinctively manly qualities.

There is truth, undoubtedly, in both these arguments; men may lose their roughness and boorishness and loud self-assertion, while they increase their self-respect, manliness and true bravery; and the testimony of Doctors Woolworth and Armstrong, and Fairchild and Hosmer, shows clearly that this latter statement expresses what has taken place where the experiment has been fairly and fully tried.

And the recent history of this country affords a valuable commentary on these statements. From no colleges did a more hardy, manly, brave body of young men go into our armies than from Oberlin and Antioch.

By that the charge of *effeminacy* is effectually dispelled.

Still another important question relates to the effect

---

* Doctor Hedge, in a recent speech at Boston.

of coëducation on young men, as regards devotion to study. On one side, it has been argued that the presence of young women would tend to divert young men from close attention to study—that it would arouse thoughts more powerful than the love of learning. On the other side, it has been argued that the desire to appear to good advantage before the young women will prove a powerful stimulus to the young men, and also that the *conscientiousness* of women in study, will certainly elevate the general tone of scholarship.

The facts, as stated by the gentlemen already referred to, and as observed by your Committee, decidedly favor the latter argument.

The next question naturally is, what is to be the effect on those it is purposed to introduce?

THE EFFECT ON YOUNG WOMEN.

The first question naturally regards the effect on *physical health.*

On one side, appear those like that eminent authority, Dr. Clarke, of Boston, who think much close study, at the time usually assigned to a college course, hurtful. These say that they are frequently called upon to treat diseases permanently injurious to body and mind brought on young women by too close application to study at this period of life.

On the other side are the statistics given by the

President of Oberlin College, and the answers given the Committee by the lady students themselves at the University of Michigan, which seem to show that the health of the young women is quite as good in college as out of it.

The deterioration in the health of American women is without doubt one of the most serious among modern social problems. It outweighs, in real importance, vast masses of questions usually claiming far more attention.

That some of this deterioration may be due to close application to study is possible, but the numbers of those who have ever closely applied themselves to study is so very small, compared with the number of those in broken health, that, evidently, search must be made for causes lying deeper and spreading wider.

The want of success in grasping and presenting these causes hitherto by men, seems to show that there should be brought to the question the instinct, the knowledge, the tact of woman herself, and it would seem that, for this, she has need of a system of education to give the mental strength required for searching out those causes, and grappling with them.

More than this, it would seem that if the cause lies to any extent in want of knowledge of great principles of health, or in want of firm character to resist the inroads of certain vicious ideas in modern civilization, a change of woman's education from its too frequent namby-pamby character, into something calculated to give firmer mental and moral texture, would help, rather than hurt in this matter.

While the Committee do not think this injury to health so likely to be increased as diminished by the system of education proposed, they hold that very careful provision should be made for the development of physical strength commensurate with mental strength.

Any college building erected for women should be planned with special reference to the health of its inmates. Sunlight should be admitted to every room and copiously; the most effective system of ventilation should be adopted; there should be a well-equipped gymnasium, and provision should be made for work in the botanical and general gardens, and for amusements.

Physiology and hygiene should be among the subjects absolutely required in every course of study.

In the general system of studies, the Committee believe that stimulus, in the way of competitive prizes, should not be brought to bear, to any considerable extent, on the young women. If any quality in their work at the various colleges, as submitted to the Committee, appears more clear than another, it is conscientiousness; and this is far more effective than emulation in its direct influence, and more responsive to considerations of health.

With such provisions and precautions, it is not likely that a body of young women would be more injured by study in the college proposed than by the aimlessness, listlessness, luxury and relaxing modes of physical and intellectual life common among young women who make no endeavor after a higher and better education.

But another class of effects claims attention—effects on *character* and *manners*.

By one side it is argued that the proposed system will probably injure the dignity, modesty, refinement and delicacy of young women,—that it will give a masculine tone.

By the other side it is argued that association, under proper restrictions, with young men engaged in scientific and literary pursuits makes any young woman feel, more than anything else, the necessity for womanly dignity and self-control, at the same time that it brings out more clearly the value of that refinement and modesty which all young men prize so highly.

That there may be some danger to certain classes of women shallow in character and weak in mind is not unlikely, but, of all women, these are the least likely to involve themselves in the labor of preparation for the university or of going on with its courses of study.

As to the good effect on the women who have actually entered the colleges, the testimony is ample. The Committee in its visits found no opposing statement either from college officers, students of either sex or citizens of university towns, and all their observations failed to detect any symptoms of any loss of the distinctive womanly qualities so highly prized.

Nor have they found that those who have been thus educated have shown any lack of these qualities in after life.

On the contrary, it would be hard to find a body of women combining these qualities more nobly than the matrons of this State and surrounding States, who have graduated at the academies and normal schools. These qualities they have, by the agreement of all observers, in a very much higher degree than the women of countries where a semi-conventual system of education is adopted.

It may be said that they must come in contact with vulgarity in words and actions, and so be injured. This, it is believed, will be rare indeed. There would at once be brought to bear a common law, a stringent code not made by any Trustees or Faculty, but none the less effective. It would be enforced by the great body of students,—and summarily. Should any boor so far forget himself, as to say or do what could be construed into an insult by the young women present, there would certainly be a sufficient number of brothers, friends or admirers of the injured parties, to take such measures as the case might demand.

And here, it may be added, would be one of the good influences on the young men. Nothing is more disheartening to those in charge of colleges, than to find profanity and obscenity, on the part of a wretched minority, tolerated by the great body of students, simply because all are men, and, by common consent, among men a man may say what he pleases.

By the admission of women the point of honor in this respect is at once changed. Words and actions before unchallenged would now be necessarily forbidden by the great body of students themselves, and such edicts would be enforced.

With the aid of a few words of common sense to young women by their matrons, and to young men by their professors, there would be created a right sentiment in this respect, powerful enough for all emergencies ; and it is believed that women would be subjected to far less annoyance from vulgarity in the university, than they constantly have to encounter in the streets or conveyances of any town or city.

It seems necessary before closing this discussion as to the effect on woman by this plan of education to allude to an argument often presented, that as woman's sphere of duty is different from that of man, her education should be different. The most natural argument from analogy would seem to destroy this position. While the physical and material duties of woman differ widely from those of men, her physical nutriment and the ordinary conditions of sound physical health are the same. The simplest analogy would lead us to the conclusion that the intellectual nutriment, and the conditions of sound mental health should be the same.

Under every roof in the land, we see persons of different sexes in the household, preparing themselves by the same diet for their different functions and duties. It would seem then that, no matter how great the difference may be between the intellectual duties and functions of the two sexes, it does not at all follow that there should be a difference in the general preliminary mental food. As the bodies of men and women are built up by the same food, whether vegetable or animal, so it would seem that their minds and hearts and souls are to be built and beautified by the same moral, mental and æsthetical food.

The very statement of this argument shows that the same education of both sexes does not lead to any usurpation of unnatural functions, social or political, by women. It would rather show that such education, by its proper development of mind and heart and soul in woman, would most surely lead to her taking that very place, and discharging best those very duties, whatever they may be, which the Creator has appointed her.

Even if the most restrictive theory of woman's duties be accepted,—even if it be allowed that her only duties are those of a well-ordered household,—would she not be fitted better for her duties as the mother of future generations of citizens by courses of study large and broad, than by the unutterable inane instructions of the great majority of our ladies' boarding and "finishing" schools?

The noble institutions of comparatively recent creation for the education of young women separately, like Vassar College and Wells College, seem to support this general line of argument by facts. The great acknowledged value of these institutions arises mainly from the fact that they have broken away from the traditions of the boarding and "finishing" schools, and have provided thorough, substantial courses of instruction more like those aimed at in our best colleges.

While the admirable character of these colleges, and the excellence of the work they are doing and will continue to do, will, doubtless, be to many an argument that young women can be most satisfactorily educated by themselves, it will be no less strong an argument for the position that, in the main, the best studies for developing the most worthy culture in young women, are identical with those required for young men.

The question now arises as to the

EFFECTS COMMON TO BOTH SEXES.

First of these is the possible formation of acquaintances likely to ripen into matrimonial engagements.

The facts conceded by President Fairchild, on this point, and his reasons based upon them have been given, and seem convincing; the Committee think that the argument may be stated in yet another way. Granting the possibility or probability of such engagements, the question comes up practically :—" How do young men and young women form such engagements *now?* "

It is matter of notoriety that these engagements—the most important of life,—are, as a rule, formed with less care, foresight and mutual knowledge, than any other. Choice is determined by mere casual meeting, by an acquaintance of a few weeks, by winning manners at a ball, by a pleasing costume in the street, and at the best by a very imperfect revelation of those mental and moral qualities which are to make or mar the happiness of all concerned. Should such engagements be formed in a university where both sexes are educated together, they would be based upon a far more thorough and extended knowledge, upon an admiration of a much higher range of qualities, and upon a similarity in taste and temper, which could not be gained elsewhere.

Every one acquainted with life in our larger and better colleges and universities, knows that nowhere do men more surely value each other for real and substantial qualities and attainments. Nowhere is the merely dressy man in lower estimation; nowhere is the thorough scholar, the ready writer, the powerful orator, more highly regarded; nowhere do wealth, family influence, intriguing, caballing, avail less; nowhere do earnest purpose and good work avail more.

Certainly the choice of a companion for life made in such an atmosphere cannot be less safe than that which is made under the present system in the world at large. If any theorist objects, with some force, that these attachments between students of either sex, would so fill the thoughts, as to leave no place for study, the testimony already laid before the Trustees shows that practical educators find that these same attachments act as a powerful stimulus to study.

And it should be remembered here, that under the

present system of separate education, attachments are frequently formed, engagements made, and the resulting correspondence kept up, and yet that this has never been considered a disturbing element in American education. On the contrary it has been generally found that young men have been steadied thereby.

Another class of effects has sometimes been feared —illicit attachments. Careful and confidential conversation and correspondence with men in position to know fully the value of this objection, fail to show any especial danger.

In the recent meeting at Boston, Dr. Edward Clarke, whose authority on any such subject is deservedly great, while opposing coëducation, on grounds alluded to elsewhere, took pains to state that immoral relations between students of a marriageable age were not feared by him. He stated distinctly that whatever danger there may be of this kind, is at an earlier period, before young women have arrived at an age to have an understanding of the necessary reserve between the two sexes. This opinion, resulting from an experience like that of Dr. Clarke who has thoroughly studied the whole question involved, both socially and physiologically, adds to the value of such testimony as that of Dr. Woolworth, who, after an experience of thirty-two years as principal of some of the largest academies in this State, in which boys and girls and young men and young women, of all ages, have been brought together, thus—according to Dr. Clarke's experience, greatly increasing the danger—uses these words:—"There have been no scandals, at least, not more than may exist between the members of a school limited to one sex and the outside world."

We would now call your attention to the

EFFECTS ON THE UNIVERSITY.

The first point that will occur to every one under this head is as to the standard of scholarship. It has been claimed, that the admission of women would tend to lower the scholarship; and no case has been more frequently cited than Oberlin College.

This objection is based upon want of recognition of the fact that Oberlin College, and others like it, carry on great preparatory schools, nominally subordinate to the regular college organization, but really outweighing it in numbers. This is not the case at the Cornell University, and there is no reason to expect that it will be. The University authorities have planted themselves firmly on the ground that they have no right to use their endowment in duplicating the instruction given in the academies and public schools.

If women shall be admitted, it will be only upon just such examinations as are passed by the young men; if they shall be continued from year to year, it will be by passing the examinations now required.

8

If it be said that the presence of women will tend to lower the standard of scholarship, or at all events to keep the Faculty from steadily raising it, it may be answered at once, that all the facts observed are in opposition to this view. The letters received by the Committee, and their own recent observations in class rooms, show beyond a doubt, that the young women are at least equals of the young men in collegiate studies. As already stated, the best Greek scholar among the thirteen hundred students of the University of Michigan, a few years since; the best mathematical scholar in one of the largest classes of that institution to-day, and several among the highest in natural science, and in the general courses of study are young women.

It has been argued that the want of accuracy and point, the "sloppiness" of much of the scholarship in some of the newer colleges, is due to the admission of women. The facts observed by the Committee seem to prove that this argument is based on the mistake of concomitancy for cause. If "sloppiness" and want of point are inadmissible anywhere, it is in translation from the more vigorous and concise ancient and modern authors. Now, the most concise and vigorous rendering from the most concise and vigorous of all—Tacitus himself—was given by a young lady at Oberlin College. Nor did the Committee notice any better work in the most difficult of the great modern languages than that of some young women at Antioch College.

Nor is our own University entirely without experience on this point. Among candidates for admission, two years since, no better examination was passed than that by a young lady who had previously been successful in a competition for the State scholarship, in one of the best educated counties of the State. That she did not remain in the Institution, was not at all due to the want of ability to compete for its higher honors.

As bearing on this point, the Committee present a letter from Professor Walter Smith, a man of great experience in England, as regards technical and art education, and who, on account of this experience, has been summoned to this country by the State of Massachusetts, and made State Director of Art Education.

"You ask my opinion, as a practical teacher, of the capacity of women and girls to take in technical education of the highest class, in arts and science, and as a corollary, what opinion I have formed of the general question, that which is now somewhat amusingly called 'the higher education of women.'

"To preface what I would say in response, I may state that for twelve years I held the position in England of Head Master of a School of Art, in the West Riding of Yorkshire, which never had less than two thousand pupils under its art instruction, (and which, for some years, had as many as six thousand pupils in its various central and district classes); also that for several years my own professional duties were spread over three schools of art, in towns—the population of which exceeded half a million—one school being a school of art and science and training-school for teachers, the only school of the kind in England, except the National Training School at South Kensington, London. The principal male and female schools of the district were also under my supervision. This, continuing in an unbroken period of ten years, gave me, as I believe, sufficient opportunities of forming an opinion upon the question of capacity for sustained study, with regard both to male and female students.

"During the period described, I must have given in the schools of art, schools and colleges in which I either taught or managed teaching, several hundreds of courses of lectures upon the subjects which lay at the foundation of a knowledge of art, and those elements of science that belong alike to art and scientific knowledge, such as geometrical drawing, orthographic projection, practical and theoretic perspective, conic sections, etc., etc., mechanical drawing being also an important subject.

"I formed a very definite opinion about the teachability of the two sexes, taught in one class, because the common evil of blackboard instruction became apparent, viz :—the teacher and all the readier pupils being made to wait until the slower ones had got through, before a fresh problem could be given. This hindrance seldom came from the female students, and did come very liberally from others. At the government examinations which came at the end of the winter course, this was more palpably shown by the results of the work done. I never remember a year in which the amount, both the prizes and certificates obtained by the ladies at these public examinations, was not, out of all proportion to the numbers competing, greater than that of those obtained by the male students.

"There is only one serious cause of failure at the public examinations at which girls sit for examination; and that is, their liability to become excited; some of the best suffer from that and are sacrificed to it.

"My opinion concerning the capacity of women to succeed in art study especially, was a good deal matured by an incident in my early experience in the north of England, which I shall not forget. When I assumed my position as Head Master, I found what probably always existed and unhapily now exists in many schools, a desire on the part of young ladies to draw and paint simple bits of prettiness, without anything educational in them. I strove hard to induce them to attack the curriculum of study of the night classes for artisans,—the school of art course,—which meant work, both physical and mental, not the coloring of bird's-nests and butterflies, etc., etc.

"At that time there were annual competitions for bronze medals awarded by the Government Art Inspectors, which were distributed by an allotment of three medals to each of twenty-three stages of instruction, *i. e.*, a possible three medals, if the work was good enough. To induce the ladies of the day classes to enter these competitions, I promised that if they would take up two stages of study, they should be reserved for them, and I would ask the male students not to compete with them. Before this, no lady had ever taken a medal in that school. Of course the result of this 'protection' was that works good enough to take all the three medals in both stages were produced. That success opened up a new world to the dozen pupils who had achieved it. The next year I declined to reserve stages for them, but recommened an open competition with the the male students in every stage. At the next annual examinations more than half the medals and prizes awarded to the school were taken by the ladies, whose numbers were about one-fifth of the numbers of the male students.

"In the following year the male students came piteously to me to ask that some of the stages of instruction might be reserved to them, *as they could not compete with the ladies.*

"Having gone through the bondage of protection and emerged into free trade, we could not go back; and since that time no reservation or distinction has been made between the students with regard to sex.

"That is an experience which will not easily be erased from my memory.

"Independently of this, I have had, in the preparation of both male and female teachers for the professional art examination at the South Kensington Museum, London, special opportunities of noting the mental capacity of both sexes in grasping purely scientific subjects, such as radial and parallel projection, and here put on record that I have found young women, not only equal to their masculine fellow students, but clearer-headed and more successful, both in their preparation and final examination in London.

"I suppose I need not refer to the comparative success of the two sexes in the more artistic subjects of study; that has been definitely settled long since in favor of the women; and it is my experience in teaching the scientific subjects as recorded above which has led me to the conclusion that in both fields, women are at least the equals of men.

"Moreover I have seen that the result of this mental work has been a very great advantage to those women who have undertaken it; it has made them happier, and by inducing a feeling of equality with their male fellow-students, has broadened their characters and increased their intelligence in everything, and thus made them more agreeable companions.

"I expect that if there be any real difference in the mental capacities of men and women, which I doubt, it will only be developed by an identical training of both, letting the results manifest themselves, without any extraneous assistance.

"It is an utterly useless experiment to teach the two sexes differently and then point to a difference of character as a proof of difference of mental capacity, which is practically what we have done in England hitherto. Up to within a year from the present time, no grammar-school in the United Kingdom was open to girls, and at the present moment no university is open to them. That is sufficient ground for asserting an entire incompetence to form an opinion on the subject, from evidence hitherto attainable of the people who allowed so gross an injustice to last so long.

"The speculations of mere theorisers on this question are absolutely worthless as evidence, and exceeding impudent in their pretentiousness.

"I have heard young men who never taught a mixed class of males and females for an hour in their lives, glibly lay down the axiom that man's is the reasoning and progressive mind, woman's the contemplative and conservative mind, and then proceed to account for this phenomenon by quotations of the opinions of philosophers, or by a recital of their own experienced observation, made probably during a ball or a picnic.

"The first thing to be done before any reliable conclusions can be come to in this matter, is to reject the evidence of those who are mere speculators or retailers of hearsay evidence. Those men and women only should be put into the witness-box who have something to say; it is utter waste of time to examine people of strong opinions, partisans of either side, who make up for their want of practical experience by great vehemence of expression.

"For my own part, I look upon a solution of this question as of more importance economically than as a matter of justice. One half of the minds of civilized people are as deliberately crippled and stunted by our foolish prejudices about capacities, as are the feet of half the Chinese crushed into shapelessness and uselessness through an old tradition. But ours is the more cruel habit of the two, for our barbarism sacrifices the beautiful mental structure; the Celestials only distort the small extremities of the body.

"Looking upon the question as one of fair play between men and women, I cannot suppose it possible for an intelligent man to believe it is for the good of the human race that the education of either half should be better than that of the other half. I am aware that some fanatical persons regard women as the superiors mentally of men, and their belief is to be accounted for by the example set to them by fanatical persons who have upheld the opposite of their creed.

"It seems to me that practical people who know anything of the subject will reject both fanaticisms and believe in the perfect equality of the two."

Still another effect upon the Institution has been prophesied by some—a loss of reputation. It is said that the admission of women would tend to its classification, in the popular mind, with certain institutions not highly esteemed among scholarly or thoughtful men, or the public at large.

That this would be the effect on some minds is probable; but the Committee see no reason to believe that this feeling would extend very far or last very long.

The same prophecies were made when the admission of young women was proposed at the University of Michigan; but the testimony of Chief Justice Cooley, a professor in that institution, shows that the standard of scholarship is not lowered, and that no permanently injurious current of opposition has been felt. The reason does not seem difficult to find. The University of Michigan was strong enough to try the experiment; it had braved storms enough not to tremble at a gust of prejudice. And it should be borne in mind that the Cornell University, too, is not so feeble in endowment, or in Faculty, or in number of students, or in the general provisions for education, or weak in its hold on the popular confidence, as to be shaken by a temporary loss of prestige in the minds of a comparatively small class.

And it should also be borne in mind that the sentiment of opposition to this movement now, is by no means so unhesitating as it was a few years since. Members of the Committee have been surprised to find many advocates of coëducation in the very quarters where they expected the most steady opposition; and even if there be opposition, all the winds of public opinion which the University has encountered thus far, have not been so favorable as to leave us without experience in buffeting opposing blasts, or, to state the fact more plainly, while no institution has ever had more noble friends or a more kindly public instinct in its favor, none has ever had to encounter a more bitter storm of misrepresentation, sneers, and old-world arguments and pedantic missiles, and it is therefore of very little consequence whether there be or be not added one more cause of futile opposition.

EFFECTS ON COLLEGES FOR THE SEPARATE EDUCATION OF WOMEN.

In view of the noble endowments and efforts already made in this State for the separate education of women, the question naturally arises, what will be the effect of the proposed experiment in coëducation upon these? Here too we can appeal to fact rather than theory. In the States where the system of educating young men and young women together is being most fully tried, there are, at the same time, institutions for the education of young women apart, flourishing and growing with the growth of the country. So it will doubtless be in the State of New York. There will always be a large number of parents who will prefer to educate their daughters in colleges like Vassar or Wells, where young women only are admitted. Nor do your Committee see anything to regret in this. That prince among modern thinkers, John Stuart Mill, never said a thing more wise than when he declared that uniformity in education is an injury, and variety a blessing. This great Commonwealth is broad enough for all, and any work proposed here will strengthen and be strengthened by all good work done at Aurora, Poughkeepsie or Elmira.

GENERAL DISCUSSION OF THE OPPOSING THEORY.

In beginning their report your Committee stated that their duty seemed first to be to investigate the facts in the case separately, then to collate them, then to throw any light thus concentrated into theories and programmes.

In accordance with this plan they would conclude the general discussion of this subject by concentrating such light as they have been able to gain, upon the main theory embedded in the arguments against mixed education.

The usual statement of this theory contains some truths, some half-truths, and some errors. As ordinarily developed, it is substantially that woman is the help-meet of man, that she gives him aid in difficulty, counsel in perplexity, solace in sorrow; that his is the vigorous thinking, hers the passive reception of such portions of thought as may be best for her; that his mind must be trained to grapple with difficult subjects, that hers needs no development but such as will make her directly useful and agreeable; that the glory of man is in a mind and heart that rejoices in solving the difficult problems, and fighting the worthy battles of life; that the glory of woman is in qualities that lead her to shun much thought on such problems, and to take little interest in such battles; that the field of man's work may be the mart or shop, but that it is well for him to extend his thoughts outside it; that the field of woman is the household, but that it is not best for her to extend her thoughts far outside it; that man needs to be trained in all his powers to search, to assert, to decide; that woman needs but little training beyond that which enables her gracefully to assent;

that man needs the university and the great subjects of study it presents; while woman needs the "finishing schools" and the "accomplishments," and that, to sum up, the character, work, training and position of women are as good as they ever can be.

The truths in this theory have covered its errors. The truth that woman is the help-meet of man has practically led to her education in such a way that half her power to aid and counsel and comfort is taken away.

The result has been that strong men, in adversity or perplexity, have often found that the "partners of their joys and sorrows" give no more real strength than would Nuremberg dolls. Under this theory, as thus worked out, the aid and counsel and solace fail just when they are most needed. In their stead the man is likely to find some scraps of philosophy begun in boarding-schools, and developed in kitchens or drawing-rooms.

But to see how a truly educated woman, nourished on the same thoughts of the best thinkers on which man is nourished, can give aid and counsel and solace, while fulfilling every duty of the household, we are happily able to appeal to the experience of many, and for the noblest portrayal of this experience ever made, we may name the dedication to the wife of John Stuart Mill of her husband's greatest essay.

But if we look out from the wants of the individual man into the wants of the world at large, we find that this optimist theory regarding woman is not supported by facts, and that the resulting theory of woman's education aggravates some of the worst evils of modern society. One of these is conventional extravagance.

Among the curiosities of recent civilization perhaps the most absurd is the vast tax laid upon all nations at the whim of a knot of the least respectable women in the most debauched capital in the world. The fact may be laughed at, but it is none the less a fact, that to meet the extravagances of the world of women who bow to the decrees of the Bréda quarter of Paris, young men in vast numbers, especially in our cities and large towns, are harnessed to work as otherwise they would not be; their best aspirations thwarted, their noblest ambitions sacrificed, to enable the "partners of their joys and sorrows" to vie with each other in reproducing the last grotesque absurdity issued from the precincts of Notre Dame de Lorette, or to satisfy other caprices not less ignoble.

The main hope for the abatement of this nuisance, which is fast assuming the proportions of a curse, is not in any church; for, despite the pleadings of the most devoted pastors, the church edifices are the chosen theaters of this display; it would seem rather to be in the infusion, by a more worthy education, of ideas which would enable woman to wield religion, morality and common sense against this burdensome perversion of her love for the beautiful.

This would not be to lower the sense of beauty and appropriateness in costume; thereby would come an æsthetic sense which would lift our best women into a sphere of beauty where Parisian grotesque could not be tolerated; thereby too would come, if at all, the strength of character which would cause woman to cultivate her own taste for simple beauty in form and color, and to rely on that, rather than on the latest whim of any foolish woman who happens to be not yet driven out of the Tuilleries or the Bréda quarter.

Still another evil in American women is the want of any general appreciation of art in its nobler phases. The number of those who visit the museums of art is wretchedly small, compared with the crowds in the temples of haberdashery. Even the love of art they have is tainted with "Parisian fashions." The painting which makes fortunes is not the worthy representation of worthy subjects; French boudoir paintings take the place of representations of what is grand in history or beautiful in legend; Wilhems and his satin dresses, Bourgereau with his knack at flesh color, have driven out of memory the noble treatment of great themes by Ary Scheffer and Paul Delaroche; Kaulbach is eclipsed by Meissonier. Art is rapidly becoming merely a means of parlor decoration, and losing its function as the embodiment of great truths.

So rapidly evaporates one of the most potent influences for good in a republic. An education of women, looking to something more than accomplishments, is necessary to create a healthy reaction against this tendency.

Still another part of woman's best and noblest influence has an alloy which education of a higher sort, under influences calculated to develop logical thought, might remove. For one of the most decided obstacles to progress of the best christian thought and right reason has arisen from the clinging of women to old abuses, and the fear of new truths. From Mary Stuart at the Castle of Ambroise to the last good woman who has shrieked against science,—from the Camarilla which prays and plots for reaction in every European court down to the weakest hunter of the mildest heresies in remote villages, the fetichisms and superstitions of this world are bolstered up mainly by women.

In Lessing's great picture, the good, kind-faced woman whose simplicity Huss blesses as she eagerly heaps up the fagots for his martyrdom, is but the type of vast multitudes of mothers of the race.

The greatest aid which could be rendered to smooth the way for any noble thinkers who are to march through the future, would be to increase the number of women who, by an education which has caught something from manly methods, are prevented from clinging to advancing thinkers or throwing themselves hysterically across their pathway.

So too that indirect influence of women on political events, so lauded even by those who are most opposed to any exercise by her of direct influence, has some bad qualities which a better system of education might diminish. The simple historical record shows that in what Bacon calls the "insanity of states," her influence has generally been direful. From Catharine de Medicis in the struggle of the League, down to Louise

Michel in the recent catastrophe at Paris—from the *tricoteuses* of the first French Revolution to the *pétroleuses* of the last, woman has seemed to aggravate rather than soothe popular fury. Nor is the history of civil strife nearer home without parallel examples.

An education which would lead women to a more thoughtful consideration of great questions and more logical treatment of them, would, perhaps, do something to aid mercy and justice in the world at those very times when they are most imperiled.

But to all this it may be said that these considerations are too general and remote—that woman's most immediate duties relate to maternity, and that her most beautiful mission relates to the dispensing of charities. As to her duties as mother, if the subject were fully discussed, it would be shown that, under the present system of physical, mental and moral education of women, there is a toleration of perhaps the most cancerous evil of modern society. Suffice it that the system of education proposed cannot make it worse, and may make it better.

As to woman's beautiful function as the dispenser of charities, it will do no harm to have leading minds among women, shown, as a stronger education would show them, that systems of charity based on impulse and not on reason have in older countries caused almost as much misery as they have cured. Her work in charity would be certainly strengthened by the training which would give her insight into this.

THE PROPOSED ENDOWMENT.

Among the matters on which the Committee was instructed to report, were any proffers of endowment having reference to the education of both sexes together.

They are now authorized to submit, herewith, the proposal signed by the Honorable Henry W. Sage, of Brooklyn, a member of the Board of Trustees, offering to the Institution the sum of two hundred and fifty thousand dollars, to be paid within three years from the acceptance of the offer, on the condition, to use his exact language, that "instruction shall be afforded to young women, by the Cornell University, as broad and as thorough as that now afforded to young men."

This is the entire statement of the condition. The Trustees are not hampered by any subordinate conditions as to method.

POSSIBLE PLANS FOR THE COEDUCATION IN THE UNIVERSITY.

In view of this offer, two plans for a Woman's College have been discussed. Both are based upon our experience, which proves that some portion of the endowment must be used in providing accommodations for boarding and lodging. Under the present circumstances of the University, remote as it is from the town, such provision is a necessity.

The first plan discussed is that of a large quadrangle or series of quadrangles adjacent to the University grounds, to be made up of a central building containing some special lecture-rooms and recitation-rooms and a museum connected with a department of botany and horticulture, and of houses, neat and well constructed, which could be afforded at a moderate rent, on condition that each tenant take into the family a certain number of lady students. Thus would be established a system akin to that of the University of Michigan,—the one which has been so long tried in the academies in this State,—that of breaking up the lady students into small colonies, and bringing them directly under family influence. The advantages of this system would be its greater economy, its smaller demands as regards supervision and its aiding to meet one of the greatest wants of the Institution,—houses for its officers and for families wishing to enjoy the benefits of a university town. Its disadvantages seem to be the difficulty of finding suitable tenants and the impossibility of the most thorough supervision by the University itself. It ought to be said, however, that it is still an open question whether this supervision is as truly effective as that exercised in the family.

The other plan, is to erect on the same land—adjacent to the University grounds—a large college building complete in all respects, with lecture-room, special recitation-rooms, infirmary, gymnasium, bathing-rooms, and study and lodging-rooms for from one hundred and fifty to two hundred lady students—a building which would form a striking architectural feature in its connection with the University.

The advantage of this new plan is that it would admit of most complete supervision—that it would tend to satisfy the popular mind in this respect and it would add to the dignity of the College and of the University. The disadvantages are that it would require the furnishing and keeping up of a great establishment.

This objection vanishes, however, before the proposed endowment, in addition to the cost of the building.

Each of these plans has strong arguments in its favor. On the side of the first may be ranged such statements of experience as those of Dr. Armstrong, Dr. Woolworth, the academies of this and surrounding States, and the University of Michigan.

On the other side is the theory of Horace Mann, who, in his letter to the Committee of the Michigan Regents, declared that a separate college-building for young women, under careful supervision, was a matter of absolute necessity; and with Mr. Mann, the great majority of the public would probably agree.

It will be observed that each plan provides for accommodation near the University buildings. This the Committee regard as absolutely essential. To place the buildings proposed at a point remote from the general University buildings, from the laboratories, the lecture-rooms, and the museums, would place the young women under great disadvantages and even dangers. It would oblige them to take long walks, and frequently, through rain and snow, after sitting in warm recitation-rooms, and this could not fail to be very injurious to their health.

It will be noted that certain lecture and recitation-rooms are provided for the young ladies under both systems. The purpose of this is two-fold :—first, there are some subjects which it may be found desirable to teach the young women apart from the young men, as for example, physiology and kindred studies. Again, there seems a peculiar fitness in bringing one leading department into especial connection with this part of the University ; this is the department of botany and horticulture. All the different plans agreed on providing a botanical lecture-room, laboratory and museum, with green house and botanical garden, in connection with the proposed College. Apart from the fact that botany and horticulture have special attractions for young women, it is believed that work in such gardens in connection with such a department would afford the best of all physical exercise.

It is not impossible, too, that, to some extent, self supporting labor may thus be afforded. The demand for floral products of every sort in all our cities is immense, and steadily increasing, and the University grounds are not more remote from some of the most important markets than are many of the existing sources of supply.

In concluding their report, the Committee would state one simple argument, which seems to them entitled to weight, even with those who dissent from many or from all of the arguments already presented.

The Cornell University is, in a certain sense a State institution. The main source of its endowment from the government of the United States and its Charter both State and National, give it this character. In view of the unmistakable tendency of popular sentiment, in view of the fact that in our Act of Incorporation, the word *persons*, referring to those entering the Institution, is to be read in connection with a context, which leads to the inference that the persons entering the University are of the same sort as the persons in the public schools and academies, that is, persons of both sexes, it seems doubtful whether it will be possible much longer to refuse to try the experiment of educating the sexes together in the University. And the the question therefore arises, whether it is not best to accept a gift which affords the best opportunity that has ever been offered to try fully and fairly the experiment. Indeed, it is a question whether we have any right to reject such an opportunity.

In view of this, as well as the considerations previously presented, your Committee recommend that Mr. Sage's gift be accepted on the conditions named by him, and that the establishment created under it be known as the Sage College of Cornell University.

ANDREW D. WHITE, *Chairman*,
In behalf of a Majority of the Committee.

www.ingramcontent.com/pod-product-compliance
Lightning Source LLC
LaVergne TN
LVHW021416110826
845150LV00007B/1944

* 9 7 8 1 4 2 5 5 0 9 6 9 9 *